WORKING WITH ADOPTIVE FAMILIES BEYOND PLACEMENT

WORKING WITH ADOPTIVE FAMILIES BEYOND PLACEMENT

Child Welfare League of America, Inc.
New York, New York

Child Welfare League of America

67 Irving Place, New York, NY 10003

Current printing (last digit)
10 9 8 7 6 5 4 3 2

Printed in the United States of America

Library of Congress Cataloging in Publication Data

Hartman, Ann.

  Working with adoptive families beyond placement.

  Bibliography: p.

  1. Adoption--United States. 2. Adoptees--United

States--Family relationships. 3. Family social work--

United States. I. Child Welfare League of America.

II. Title.

HV875.64.H37 1984   362.8'2   84-1850
ISBN 0-87868-219-8

ABR 2786

ACKNOWLEDGMENTS

This publication is part of a project of the National Adoption Information Exchange System (NAIES), under the auspices of the Child Welfare League of America, pursuant to HHS Contract No. 105-79-1102.

Originally intended for publication by the U.S. Department of Health and Human Services, Office of Human Development Services, Administration for Children, Youth and Families, Children's Bureau, this publication was subsequently released by HHS, making possible its publication by the Child Welfare League of America in cooperation with the National Child Welfare Training Center, School of Social Work, University of Michigan.

CONTENTS

I. INTRODUCTION

Permanency for Children

The past decade has witnessed a virtual revolution in the field of child welfare. This revolution has grown out of a major reexamination of the child welfare system which took place in the 1960s and early 1970s. Several things sparked this searching critique of child welfare services.

First, new X-ray technology and the use of X-rays in the evaluation of injured children gradually led to the identification of the battered child syndrome and to a growing awareness of and alarm about the extent of child abuse taking place in American homes and institutions.[1] Secondly, a series of research projects began to surface information about the numbers of children growing up in long-term foster care.[2] The public began to be aware of the fact that many children were lost in this system, growing up in multiple, relatively unsupervised foster homes, alienated from biological kin, and having no permanent ties with a substitute family.

Thirdly, the advocacy and human rights movements of the 1960s and early 1970s spread to the consideration of the rights of children. It became apparent that children inadequately nurtured or protected by their parents cannot advocate for themselves and can become among the most oppressed, abused, and neglected groups in our society.

A range of citizen groups organized themselves around child advocacy issues, pressing for better protection for and services to children. These included such important groups as the Children's Defense Fund, North American Center on Adoption, National Commission on Children in Need of Parents, and New York Citizen's Committee for Children. The demands for change from such advocacy groups as well as from many professionals concerned with the quality of services to families and children has given great impetus for the reform of the child welfare system.

One of the results of these far-ranging knowledge development and advocacy efforts was the final passage into law of 96-272, the Child Welfare and Adoption Reform Act of 1980. This legislation has many components but its major thrust is to enhance and support the goal of permanence for all children. By permanence, it is meant that every child has a right to a permanent home with a family.

The first tenet of this guiding philosophy in child welfare is that every effort must be made to maintain children in their own homes through the support and rehabilitation of the biological family and to return children who have been placed to their biological parents when this is at all possible.

The second principle of this position is that if a child is unable to be reunited with his or her biological family, then a permanent family should be found for him or her through adoption. The permanency movement, led by such groups as the North American Center on Adoption and the National Commission on Children in Need of Parents, had thus redefined the concept of the "adoptable child." Until a decade ago, most children over two or three years of age or children with any kind of physical or emotional handicap or even children with unknown or supposedly undesirable hereditary backgrounds were considered unadoptable. Clearly, the clients of such practice were the adoptive families, and child welfare agencies attempted to make assurance to these families about the health and potential of infants they adopted far beyond any assurances a biological family can have when they give birth to a child. The redefinition of the notion of the adoptive child has led to a conviction that has become at once a call to arms and a goal: "No child is unadoptable."

This major change in child welfare policy and goals has required far-reaching changes in the delivery of services to children. It leads to a changing view of the total adoptive process including new approaches to recruitment, to assessment, and to the preparation of children and parents for adoption.

A Changing View of Postplacement Services

One of the areas that requires the most change in the new conceptualization of adoption practice is the whole area of the postplacement services. In infant adoption, postplacement services were rather minimal. They often consisted of perfunctory visits for a period of up to a year for the purpose of monitoring how things were going with the new family. It was anticipated that young couples with their new babies would not have any particular difficulty. Adoptive couples, who had often gone through a rather searching evaluative process by the agency to determine whether they were potentially adequate parents, and who were anxious to prove themselves as good parents during this probationary period before the finalization of the adoption, were understandably unlikely to talk with the agency worker about problems, concerns, insecurities and anxieties as they emerged.

Postplacement services in this new model of adoption are built on the assumption that families will need help at times, in the months and even years following adoption. It is assumed that the family and the children are taking on complex and difficult changes in their lives and that there will be rough spots when an outside person who has special knowledge about this building process can be of help. In no way in this model are difficulties during the postplacement period considered to be a failure or problem on the part of either the family or the child but an understandable accompaniment of a challenging and unique life situation.

Secondly, in order for families to be able to make use of the adoption worker or another staff member in the agency for help in dealing with the new adoption, the whole concept of the "probationary" period following the placement must be altered or families will be reluctant to risk sharing with the agencies. This change must reach back into the "home study" period. Heavily evaluative home studies

2

establish a particular kind of relationship between the potential adoptive family and the agency. This relationship is characterized by a judgemental attitude on the part of agency and worker, no matter how well disguised, and is almost the opposite of the atmosphere of acceptance and unconditionality which forms the basis of a helping relationship.

Adoptive families have reported time and time again how defensive they felt and how agonizing the home study process was. Once this kind of relationship has been established with the agency through the early part of the contact, it is very hard to change that relationship and to encourage families to seek postadoptive services from the agencies. Therefore, in order for postadoptive services to be successful, an initial change must take place in the home study process so that the families will not hide their concerns and will be willing to share their problems. Defensiveness on the part of families leads them to define difficulties as the result of immutable negative characteristics within the child.

Good postadoption service must be based on a home study and on a relationship between the adoptive families and the agency that has been open and sharing and where the decision to proceed with the adoption has come out of a shared decision-making process in which both agency and family actively participated. A model of this kind of family assessment process appears in a monograph previously prepared by the author.[3] In some ways the present work can be considered a companion to that volume.

Finally, a reconceptualization of postplacement services in this new revolution in adoption requires that postadoption services be available on an as-needed basis throughout the growing-up period of the child.

Such ongoing services would also have been useful for infant adoptions as the status of the adoptee and the adoptive parent does have different characteristics than biological parenthood and childhood. At various key times throughout the developmental cycle of the child and of the family the issue of adoption emerges and puts special demands on both child and family. For example, emerging concerns about identity and identity formation during a child's adolescent years frequently reawaken interest in biological roots and child and family may well need help in dealing with this. The search movement has underlined the specialness of the adoptive status and the fact that, for many, the connection of the biological family is never totally severed even for an adoptee who has been relinquished and adopted in the early weeks of life.

Agencies have been more ready to recognize that families who adopt children who are older and bring with them scars of painful early life experiences, families that adopt children with special needs, may require ongoing help. The combined effects of the search movement and the changing views of adoption have led agencies to begin to offer longer term and more extensive postadoption services.

3

The Child Welfare League of America's Standards for Adoption Services (p. 50) states that "the purpose of postplacement services should be to offer help, as needed and desired by the family, in both development of the parent-child relationship and in the resolution of problems inherent in adoption."

This monograph presents a model of working with families after adoptive placement in terms of the development of the relationships between the family members and the child and the integration of the child into the family. We also focus on approaches to dealing with some special issues and tasks that emerge for families who are formed through adoption.

Our presentation begins with identifying some of the special aspects of adoption as a family-building process. We then move on to present an ecologically oriented family-centered approach to working with families after placement. We emphasize specific strategies for helping families in the first weeks and months after placement, when family and child are struggling with the tasks and changes involved in the child becoming an integral part of the family. We focus on a model that can be used by the worker with a family, but also discuss group and self-help approaches.

Finally, we discuss long-term postadoption services, indicating when in the life cycle and in what format these might be offered.

II. BUILDING A FAMILY THROUGH ADOPTION

The process of attachment of parents to child starts in pregnancy. In fact, it probably starts far before pregnancy in the fantasies and the discussions of the potential parents. More and more attention has been paid recently to facilitating the process of attachment from pregnancy through birth and in the hours and days beyond birth. Preventive mental health practitioners and medical staffs have studied ways to handle the birthing and postpartum period in such a way as to enhance the mother/child and father/child bonding. The return to nursing, the inclusion of the father, rooming-in plans, births at home, and natural childbirth, which enables the mother to be awake during the birth process and thus immediately aware of and available to the baby, have all been steps that have potential for strengthening the attachment and bonding process. A major thrust has been to keep professionals and institutional arrangements from standing between parents and child and interfering with the natural bonding processes as they have in the past.

Biological family membership and entitlement are clear and socially supported so that a child "belongs" to a family. Parents, through conception and birthing, are "entitled" to be the child's parents. This sense of belonging and entitlement gives the parents the right to feel secure about caretaking, about decision making, about taking responsibility for rearing and for the future of the child. On the other hand, children, through their sense of belonging to a family, feel entitled to care, nurture, support, and to more subtle things like knowing who they are. The old definition of a family expresses this: "A family is the folks that have to take you in when you've got no place else to go."

Bonding, belonging, and entitlement and the social processes that promote and enhance them form a basis for the powerful cohesion that exists in families. They are a part of the structure of emotional ties and socially sanctioned reciprocal roles, duties, and obligations that describe "families."

The whole process of building a family through adoption is very different than becoming a family through biological parenting. In a sense, adoption can be more accurately likened to marriage as a way of forming a family. Marriage is not a biological event. It is a social event in which two people who are biologically unrelated become family, because, in most cases, they have made a choice to do so. Becoming a family through marriage happens through a legal procedure and a socially sanctioning ritual, which announces the rights, obligations, connections and commitment which now and henceforth exist between the married pair. In adoption, we have always used biological birth as a model. Perhaps it would be more useful to think about marriage as a metaphor for adoption rather than birthing. In a sense, those two ways of making a family are much more alike.

As in marriage, in adoption the process of building attachment, a sense of belonging, and entitlement take place over days, months, and years. It starts during the decision-making period when the family and an agency are working together to decide whether adoption makes sense for this family. It continues through the selection period which hopefully involves the active handling of the placement process. Throughout every phase of adoption the question should always be asked: "How can the building of attachment, the building of sense of belonging, and the building of sense of entitlement be facilitated?" This is also the question that gives direction to postadoption services.

The Acceptance of Difference

One of the key issues in working through the adoption process and in the long run in determining whether or not the adoption will be successful is whether the adoptive family and the child can accept the difference between adoption and building a family biologically.

David Kirk, in his study of adoption, Shared Fate (1964), discovered that the single variable that was most influential in determining whether an adoption was successful was whether the adoptive family could accept that difference. Unfortunately, adoption agencies in the past have frequently been in collusion with adoptive couples in an effort to deny the difference between adoptive family building and biological family building. The guiding principle of adoption practice was to make adoption as much as possible like biological parenting. This denial of difference, which of course is a denial of reality, creates a number of problems for the family and for the child who is adopted. Where there is a denial of difference, there is also a denial of biological ties. This includes the denial of the children's interest in or attachment to any figures that existed in their lives previous to the point of their adoption. The denial of difference really requires a cutting off of the former life of the child and the child's previous experience. By modeling adoption after birth, the illusion is preserved that the child was born the day that he or she came to the family.

Another outcome of the denial of difference has been that the agency has removed itself from the adoption process as quickly as possible. As soon as the adoption agency is out of the picture, the family can then be like any other family and the special status of being an adoptive family is denied. Along with that denial is the view that an adoptive family has no special needs or special issues to be dealt with that are different from issues and needs to be found in biologically formed families.

The denial of difference has denied to the adoptive parents the fact that they may indeed have some difficulties in dealing with the special status of adoption in the future and has left them feeling that if they do have any problems, it is somehow related to their own insufficiencies or to defects in the child and not to the fact that the status of adoption is a special status that has special needs and requires special handling throughout life. Families that have difficulties in the years following adoption may find themselves seeking help in mental health agencies where the staff has no knowledge of adoption and, in fact, often consider the fact that the child has been adopted as inconsequential or irrelevant to the

6

problems at hand. Even if mental health workers are aware of the fact that the child was adopted and consider that it might have some importance, they have little knowledge or experience as to what this means in the family system.

In infant adoptions it has perhaps been easier for agencies, parents, and adoptees to deny the differences between adoption and biological parenting as the placement of the child at a few days or weeks old or more easily simulates biological parenting. However, these differences do continue to exist and adoptees and their families have paid their price for this denial. The nature of this ongoing denial is illustrated in the following vignette. The author was conducting a workshop for professionals on working with families and the issue of adoption came up. There was considerable discussion about the importance of biological ties and on the search movement. Following the workshop a young man approached me and said "I hate to disabuse you of your ideas about biological ties, but I want you to know that I am adopted and I have absolutely no interest in my real family." While denying his interest in his biological roots, without being aware of it, he terms them his "real" family.

In the adoption of special needs children, of children that are primarily older, it is much harder to deny the difference between adoption and biological parenting. And in fact it has been found that families that have chosen to adopt special needs children have had less need to deny difference.[4] It may well be that parents who elect to adopt these special needs and older children have less need to replicate the biologically formed family and are able to accept building a family through adoption as a special way of creating a family with its own character, needs, requirements, and positives.

Families who can understand and accept the differences between biological parenting and adoption and who can accept the child's background, "have taken a giant step toward preventing: a.) a negative self-image of the child based on lack of information about his history; b.) breakdown in family communication because the child's questions are unwelcomed and unanswered; c.) bitterness and self-hate in the child who conceives his/her antecedents as unacceptable; and d.) the child's ultimate disappointment in the adoptive parents because of their unresponsiveness to the need to know about biological origins."

Such parents can also recognize that in this special family building process, they may well encounter special problems and experience special needs and are able to turn to the agency for help.[5]

Separation and Attachment

Issues around separation and attachment also have special meaning and consequences for adoptive families. Love at first sight is a cherished fantasy in the American culture both in romance and between parents and children. Somehow the expectation is that there should be instant love, instant caring and bonding. Children, of course, are supposed to love their parents and parents are supposed to love their children. In adoptive families where there has been a denial of

7

difference, that is, where fantasies about instant love and about unambivalent attachment prevail, there can be a good deal of guilt and anxiety and sense of self-blame about the fact that instant love doesn't happen in adoption and that caring and bonding, that the development of attachment, take a long time.

Older and special needs children are frequently troubled, angry, and distant. They may be unresponsive, violent, uncontrollable. They frequently are, at times, very unlovable, leaving adoptive parents feeling disappointed, helpless, impotent, and frustrated. Often adoptive parents go through periods of even disliking the child they have brought into their home. The problem that must be dealt with, however, is not the fact that the adoptive parent has negative feelings about the child, but rather, they may need some help about the guilt they may feel in response to these negative feelings. The denial of difference between adoptive and biological parenting can accentuate these feelings of guilt, which can be considerably more destructive than the negative feelings themselves.

From the child's point of view, there are different issues related to attachment. Some children, the more fortunate ones, have been deeply attached to a previous family, perhaps in a foster home. Such children have to deal with their feelings of loss, of change, and the pain and difficulty of having to become attached to a new family. The process of placement, visiting back and forth, ongoing contacts with the foster parents and important kin can help the child make the transition from the old to the new family. Although the move may be painful for the child who has loved and who has been loved in the previous homes, it will be easier for this child to attach to the new family than for a child who has not experienced love and security. An important variable in determining the success of the transition is the adoptive family's ability to support the prior attachment. If they have a need to disqualify it, to undermine it, and invalidate it, or to act as if it never existed, the child will feel invalidated, will bury his or her feelings, and fail to work through the loss.

The maintenance of the earlier ties will make it much more possible for the child to form new ties. Further, if the family is positive, supportive, and sharing with important figures in the child's life, the child will be less likely to "blame" the adoptive family for any feelings of deprivation or the pain of separation.

More frequently in the case of the special needs child, particularly the child who has been considered emotionally impaired, he or she has been moved from home to home, perhaps has come from an abusive home, is distrustful of adults and of promises of "You are here to stay." The repeated experiences of having been moved in response to his or her difficult behavior leaves the child expecting, anticipating, and often provoking being rejected in a new home.

The honeymoon period can communicate false optimism to the adoptive parents. This superficial period of tranquility occurs only because the child is remaining unattached. The honeymoon ends when the child begins to feel stirrings of caring and longing which bring back the old pain that he or she has experienced in relation to adults and to rejection. The child's response to these stirrings is to fight the attachment, to be hostile and negative, or to begin a long period of testing to demonstrate that the family, like all other families, will not be able to or willing to "hang in there" with the child. If children anticipate rejection and being sent away, they will tend to precipitate this to deal with the anxiety about waiting for it to happen. As adoptive parents do not respond to this period of testing by rejecting the child, he or she may escalate the testing and become even more anxious because this different kind of response is confusing and frightening. In general, the child would rather be sent back, sent away, than risk becoming attached and be sent away later.

This tumultuous period can be reframed for the family as a demonstration of the fact that the child is beginning to care. The more intense the testing the more likely it is the child is experiencing a growing temptation to begin to attach. Going through the testing period, sharing the pain of loss and uncertainty with the child, surviving and staying with the child through a tantrum, all facilitate bonding and attaching.[6] All of us have experienced how quickly bonding takes place when an intense experience is shared. Often people will say of a close and committed relationship, "We have been through a lot together." The painful experiences in the first days and weeks and months of placement offer the adoptive parents an opportunity to hang in there with the child through the pain and anger and frustration. Sharing these times and refusing to back off not only reassures children that the parents accept them and will be there for them but also forms the basis in shared experience of real bonding.

Entitlement

Those interested in understanding the process of family building through adoption have identified the concept of entitlement as useful in thinking about what happens in the adoption process.[7] Entitlement is taken for granted in biological families. The right of family members to make claims upon one another and to expect from one another is a part of being a family and is strongly socially supported.

For the child, issues of entitlement, issues of belonging to a family, raise issues of loyalty. Am I entitled to membership in this family? Does belonging to this family mean that I do not belong to my previous family? Can I be entitled to belong to this family when I haven't been born into it and still have feelings about other adults? All of these issues emerge over the entitlement issue, standing between the child and his or her ability to make a commitment to the family.

The family struggles with the same issue. Can they and do they feel entitled to be the parents of this child? The whole adoption process is a long and often drawn out entitlement process, beginning with the study phase which families often interpret as an examination to determine if they are good enough to be entitled to have a child. The sense of being on probation which grows out of the fact that finalization of adoption is usually postponed for a year communicates the same kind of feeling. The family is on trial. They are on probation to determine

9

whether they are entitled to be parents. The way the study period is handled
the way the actual placement takes place, the attitude of the worker and
agency toward the adoptive family and their rights to have a child, can hav
powerful impact on the parent's growing sense of entitlement. If the agency
worker take a proprietary air and act as if they "own the child," entitlement on
part of the adoptive parents will be slow in developing. Further, the helplessn
that the adoptive parents feel in dealing with problems and issues as they arise w
the child also can undermine the sense of entitlement. In a sense, the adopt
parents can feel that if they do not know how to handle a youngster, they have
right to be his or her parents. The agency's response to the family's need,
extent to which the agency is reassuring and supportive, making use of the far
strengths in solving the problems, in part determines the family's feelings
entitlement.

We now turn to a more extensive and specific presentation of an ecologically
oriented family systems approach to helping families following adoptive placement.
Throughout our discussion, we will return time and again to these special issues in
building a family through adoption, issues of separation and attachment, of
entitlement and belonging, and to the importance of recognizing the differences
between adoption and biological parenting.

III. AN ECOLOGICALLY ORIENTED FAMILY SYSTEMS APPROACH TO HELPING FAMILIES

The assessment and interventive strategies presented in this monograph are based on an ecological perspective on social work practice and on an understanding of and approach to the family as a system.

The science of ecology studies the sensitive balance that exists between living things and their environments and the ways in which this mutuality may be enhanced and maintained. Social workers have recently attempted to use the ecological metaphor to provide a new way of thinking about and understanding what has always been a central focus in social work: person-in-situation.

In organizing our approach to helping families through postplacement services, we will consider the family in three dimensions. First, we will look at the family relationship with its ecological world and consider that relationship as primary target for change. We will then look at the family as a system. We will look at the structure of the family, at how it has been impacted by the addition of a new member, and at the interpersonal processes that are impacted by the adoptive status. We will then look at the family through time, study, and mapping the intergenerational family history so that the possibility that some intergenerational issues are having their impact on the family's current responses to the adoptive situation and to the adopted child may be explored.

In considering each one of these dimensions, we will present some organizing concepts and some practical tools to sharpen and enhance a worker's ability--not only to understand what is happening in the family, but also to devise some specific strategies for change and help which can grow out of that understanding. Throughout, our approach will be family-focused and for the most part will center on work with the total family unit or with the adoptive parents. Our bias is to avoid working directly with the adopted child, not only because we consider postadoption integration and adaptation as family matters but also because direct work with the child tends to undermine the parent's sense of being "in charge," of being competent, in short, of entitlement.

The Family in Crisis

In assessing and helping the family in postadoption services during the first days and weeks and even months following placement, it is useful to consider that the family may well be in crisis.[8] This kind of assessment leads to an understanding that the family is not presenting chronic dysfunctional patterns but rather the difficulties being experienced are reactive to the adoptive placement, to the new demands being made on the family, to precipitous life-style changes, and to rapid alterations in the structure of the family relationship system.

Every young couple, in giving birth to a biological child, has experienced the rapid and often overwhelming changes that take place when they begin their role as parents. Even though there has been preparation for these changes for many months before the arrival of the newborn, their world is often turned upside down. What was a couple becomes a three-person system and that new third person powerfully affects the organization of that system and the relationship between the family and the outside world. The demand for change can overwhelm a couple's adaptive capacities; can cut off sources of nurture, stimulation, and support; and often leaves a young family in a state of crisis. The delicate balance between the family and its world and within the family system is upset.

The addition of an adopted child to a family has many of the same effects. Whether it is a first child, a third, or a fifth, the entry of any new member into a family demands change. It is these demands for change placed on the system that tax adaptive capacities and develop stress. The nature of these changes, the impact of the adoption on both the inner family system and the family's relationship with its world, must be understood. Helping efforts are directed toward a restoration of the balance between the family and its world, a reduction of stress, and a creative adaptation to change and to new demands.

As we consider each dimension, as we look at the family in space, at the family through time, and inside the family system, we ask, "How have things changed? What old patterns and adaptations have ceased to be viable? What effort is the family making to restore a balance? Where are the areas of stress, discomfort, and conflict? What kinds of shifts might be made to restore a comfortable and productive balance?

IV. THE FAMILY IN ITS WORLD

The first dimension to examine is the family's relationship with its world. As we turn, however, to examine this complex ecological system, we are faced with an overwhelming amount of interrelated data. We want to be able to get a picture of the family and the environment, and of the relationships between these systems. We want to focus on the sources of nurture, stimulation, and support from the intimate and extended environment as well as on deficits, needed resources, and sources of stress and conflict.

The Eco-Map[9] was devised as an interviewing, assessment, and integrative tool to capture and organize this complexity. It is a paper-and-pencil simulation which can be constructed with the total family or in interviewing one member, and helps the family or family member observe and reflect upon the current quality of their life space. Of course, in postadoptive services, the question is always, "How has this map changed since the placement?" Doing the Eco-Map with the family helps them consider what these changes have been, which ones are stressful, which ones have meant that the family has lost an important source of nurture, and which new connections have added stimulation and interest to the family. In doing the Eco-Map, the opportunity to view the family in its life space is shared by worker and family and gives them an opportunity to objectify this complex system and to discuss it. Families are often unaware of the kinds of change that have occurred in their relationships with their world since the placement of a child in their home as they have been preoccupied with the tasks and the excitement and the interest involved in the new relationship. The map helps them become more aware of these changes and to take control and to master the nature of their relationship with their world.

The Eco-Map is a drawing that maps in a dynamic way the ecological system boundaries which encompass the family in the life space. Included in the map are the major systems which are part of the family's world and the nature of the family's relationships with these various systems. The Eco-Map portrays an overview of the family and their situation. It pictures the important nurturing or conflict-laden connections between the family and the world, and points to conflicts to be mediated, bridges to be built, and resources to be sought and mobilized.

Instructions for Eco-Mapping

An Eco-Map may be done with an empty piece of paper, or it may be constructed by completing a blank Eco-Map similar to the one that follows. Each procedure has certain advantages. Starting without any structure may lead to somewhat more flexibility. Use of the structured map, however, is a time-saver and also quickly suggests to those participating what the procedure is all about. It may be easier to learn Eco-Mapping by following the structured map.

Figure I   Name _____
                                 Date _____

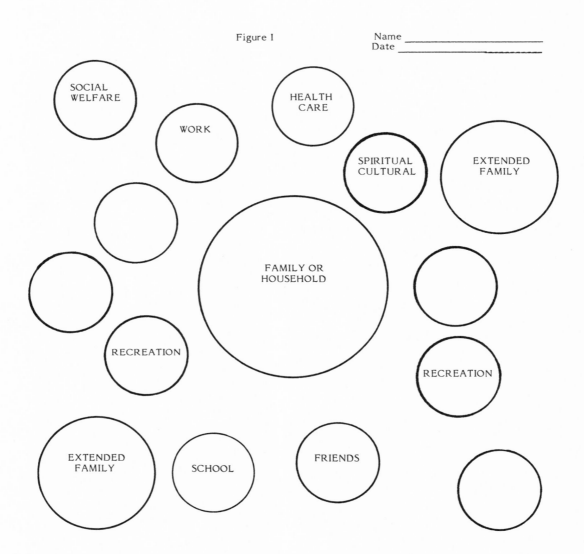

Fill in connections where they exist.
Indicate nature of connections with a descriptive word or by drawing different kinds of
     lines: _____ for strong, ---------- for tenuous, ⫫⫫⫫⫫ for stressful.
Draw arrows along lines to signify flow of energy, resources etc. → →
Identify significant people and fill in empty circles as needed.

14

Within the large circle in the middle of the Eco-Map, chart the members of the household. This is done as follows: a woman is indicated by a circle; a man by a square.

A married couple is portrayed as follows:

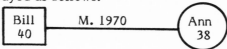

It is often useful to add their names and ages. Perhaps Bill and Ann have two sons, also living in the home.

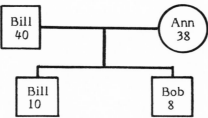

Ann's mother came to live with them after her father died.

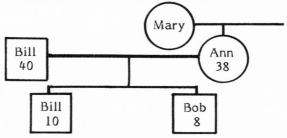

This, then, is a picture of the household. The usefulness of pictures is already demonstrated when one considers the number of words it would take to communicate the facts represented in the Eco-Map.

A single parent, divorced, mother of one son and living with her parents would be pictured as follows:

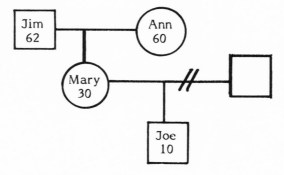

The mapping of more complex family systems is demonstrated in the discussion of genograms that follows.

Having pictured the household within the large circle in the middle of the Eco-Map, the next step is to begin to draw in the connections between the family and the different parts of the ecological environment. Some of the most common systems in the lives of most families, such as work, extended family, recreation, health care, school, and so on, have been labeled in the blank map. Other circles have been left undesignated so that the map is sufficiently flexible to be individualized for different families.

Connections between the family and the various systems are indicated by drawing lines between the family and those systems. The nature of the connection may be expressed by the type of line drawn. A solid or thick line indicates an important or strong connection. A broken line indicates a tenuous connection. A hatched line shows a stressful or conflicted relationship. It is also very useful to indicate the direction of the flow of resources, energy, or interest by drawing arrows along the connections lines.

In testing out the Eco-Map, we have found that the use of the three kinds of lines for conflicted, strong, and tenuous relationships is an efficient shorthand when the worker uses the Eco-Mapping procedure as an analytic tool without the family's direct participation. When using the map as an interviewing tool, however, this type of line code has often been felt to be too constraining. Workers prefer to ask families to describe the nature of the connection and then to qualify that connection by writing a descriptive word or two along the connecting line.

Some of the connections may be drawn to the family or household as a whole when they are intended to portray the total group's relationship with some system in the environment. Other connections may be drawn between a particular individual and an outside system when that person is the only one involved, or different family members are involved with an outside system in different ways. This differentiation enables the map to highlight contrasts in the way various family members are connected with the world.

It is easy to learn to do the Eco-Map, and it is important to become comfortable with it before using it with adoptive applicants. A simple way to learn is to do one's own Eco-Map. It is also useful to practice with a friend or two.

Use of the Eco-Map in Postadoption Services

The primary value of the Eco-Map is the visual impact it has and its ability to organize and present concurrently a great deal of factual information. The visual examination of the map has considerable influence on the way both the worker and the family perceive the situation. The connection and themes and the quality of the family's life seem to jump off the page and lead to a more holistic and intergrated perception. The value of the map was demonstrated in the comment a twelve-year-old boy made upon looking at his map, "Gee, I never saw myself like that before."

There are special ways the Eco-Map can be used in postadoption services. If, for example, the preadoption assessment process was done by the same model as presented in this monograph, a very dramatic way to determine the kinds of changes that have taken place since the placement is simply to construct a new map and then to compare it with the map that was done during the assessment period. This before-and-after opportunity clearly demonstrates the way the addition of a new member to the family has made a major change in the family's relationship with the environment.

Often, however, such a map will not be available, and therefore, an understanding of how the current situation has changed can take place through a review of the map and through discussion. For example, has some source of gratification or stimulation that was an important part of the family's life been eliminated since the placement of the child? Any child moving into a family makes certain demands and certainly the first months of the placement of an older child with special needs will make considerable demands on the family members. The question then emerges, what has been the impact of these demands? This must particularly be considered in relationship to the mother in the family. In our culture, despite changes that are occurring, women do tend to take the major responsibility for child care. Have the demands for child care cut her off from the things that were important to her? Is she seeing friends, is she continuing with her social connectedness? Was there a hobby or activity that was important to her that she has given up? The same thing can be asked of children in the family. Particularly in the early phases of adoption, one child in particular in the family may have taken over responsibility for being with and relating to the adoptive child. Certainly such an impulse on the part of the children in the family is positive and helpful. However, if they have cut off from their friends or limited some of their important activities, if they have sacrificed too much to involve themselves with the new member of the family, in the long run resentment and regret are almost inevitable. In doing maps with families, the mother may say, "I didn't realize it, but do you know I haven't been bowling or to one of my church circle meetings since Johnny came!"

The worker's stance in discussing these kinds of changes must be to examine what it is like for family members to have made these changes and to wonder if there are not some ways that important nurturing and stimulating relationships with the systems in the ecological environment could be reactivated. Frequently, families who adopt are child-centered---but child-centeredness has its limits. In their wish to do a good job and to attend to the needs of their new member, family members may have become excessively child-centered and given up external connections in favor of devoting too much of their time to the child. The Eco-Map leads to problem solving around how important external connections can be maintained and the tasks of the home managed. As the family views the map together, the shifts and sacrifices attendant to taking the child into the home cease to be hidden sources of anger and disappointment. Rather, they become topics for problem solving and planning among the group as a whole.

A second area for exploration relates to the amount of stress that the family is dealing with in their ecological environment. Children who come into adoptive homes often require special trips to medical care, planning for special education in school systems, and other resource mobilization. This increase in stress should be noted and ways of both mastering and distributing stress among family members discussed. Again the worker can observe the map with the family and comment, "There seems to be a lot of stress. There are a lot of arrows going out at this point and not much coming in." The family can talk together about rectifying this balance.

The possibilities for problem solving in terms of stress or in terms of the family's relationship with their environment are many. Perhaps some other helping resources could be made available. Perhaps father could take over part of the caretaking functions usually handled by mother to allow her time to pursue some of her old interests. Perhaps the children should be freed from at least part of their obligations to their new sibling and perhaps the adopted child can be helped to develop appropriate extra family resources so that he or she is not so dependent on the family for all of his or her nurture and support.

Finally, the Eco-Map not only clarifies the family's relationship with school, work, health care, and other more distant systems, it also portrays the extent to which family members are connected with an intimate network including extended family and friends. In a recent research study it was discovered that families who adopt older children and children with special needs are likely to meet with negative responses and lack of encouragement and support from kin and friends. "Being innovators in family behavior, they appear to be subject to the ridicule and condemnation those in the vanguard of any social movement are likely to incur."[10]

The Eco-Map surfaces the extent to which the family is in touch with extended family and friends and provides an opportunity to discuss these important relationships. Has the family felt criticized and have they pulled back from social connectedness? Have they helped others to understand, giving them the opportunity to adapt to the change and to share? Evidence that the family's social network has shrunk just when there is a need for support and validation is crucial information. Social support and reinforcement is an important component of the parents' sense of entitlement. If friends and family are not supportive or are even critical of the adoption, this can undermine their developing sense of family and can promote social isolation.

Simply surfacing the fact that the intimate social network is deteriorating and encouraging the family to talk about this can be an important intervention. It may be important for one or another of the parents to meet alone and discuss the issue with an important extended family member. This kind of intervention will be discussed in more detail when we explore intergenerational issues.

An elaborate and powerful intervention which can bring about major changes within the family emotional system and in the family's relationship with its social network is the adoption ritual. This will be discussed in detail in our presentation of change strategies utilized to alter the family relationship system.

The use of the Eco-Map with the family provides a good way to begin postadoption services. It presents an overview of the family in its environment and makes obvious some practical ways of dealing with the changes that have developed in the family's relationship with its world. It also expands the potential areas of interest and concern, focusing on relationships with the world, on the environment, and on possible external stresses rather than assuming that the tension and difficulties are necessarily to be found in some defect within the child or failure of the parents.

Harold and Bess Davies adopted 7-year-old Peter. Peter had been severely neglected by his teenage biological mother and was removed from his home through protective services at age 2½. He made good adjustment in his first home, but was abruptly replaced after four months when the foster mother became ill. After a three-month stay in a second home, he was returned to his biological mother for several months. Again, he suffered from neglect and there was suspicion that he had been abused by the mother's boyfriend. He was again placed and before termination of the mother's rights could be completed, she left the state. Two years and two foster homes later, Peter was finally free for adoption, but by then, he was identified as "emotionally impaired" and there was considerable concern about whether he could make it in an adoptive home. He was finally placed with a very experienced and skillful foster mother and he improved to the point that the agency began to consider adoption. He was placed with the Davies who had two daughters, eleven and nine years old. After two rather calm months, tension began to build in the family. Peter was reverting to some of his old behavior, he and the nine-year-old were fighting a good deal, and Bess was feeling distressed and discouraged. The worker met with the whole family together. They constructed the Eco-Map shown in Figure 2.

Several things emerged during the Eco-Mapping sessions that contributed to an understanding of the mounting tension in the family, tension that Peter was probably responding to as accurately as a barometer does to weather changes. First, it became clear that Bess, who had been very active in the community, had withdrawn from many of her activities. Both parents expressed a strong reluctance to use a sitter at this point. Two efforts to go out alone and to leave the children with former sitters had not worked out as Peter had been so upset. This meant that one of the parents had to be home after school and in the evening.

Two things had recently happened in Harold's life that had altered the family's situation. First, shortly after Peter was placed, Harold's mother, who had always been independent and self-sufficient, had suffered a serious stroke and was now in a nursing home. An only child, Harold had to assume total responsibility for arranging for his mother's care and was also visiting her every Sunday afternoon.

19

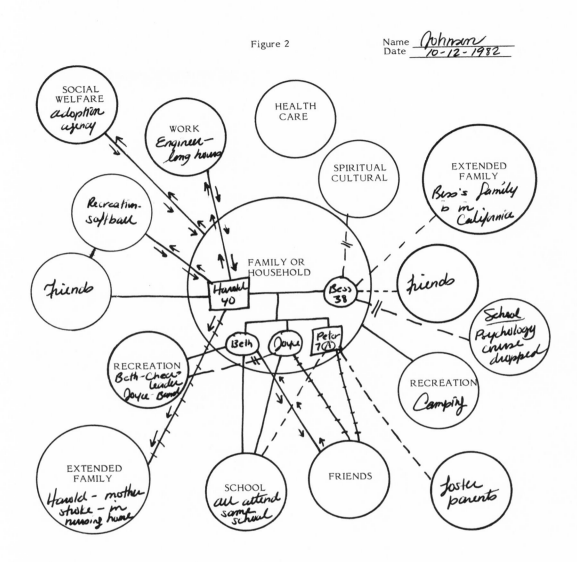

Figure 2

Name *Johnson*
Date *10-12-1982*

SOCIAL WELFARE — *adoption agency*

WORK — *Engineer — long hours*

HEALTH CARE

SPIRITUAL CULTURAL

EXTENDED FAMILY — *Bess's family in California*

Recreation — *softball*

FAMILY OR HOUSEHOLD

Harold 40 *Bess 38*

friends

friends

School Psychology course dropped

Beth *Joyce* *Peter 7*

RECREATION — *Beth - Cheerleader Joyce - Band*

RECREATION — *Camping*

EXTENDED FAMILY — *Harold - mother stroke - in nursing home*

SCHOOL — *all attend same school*

FRIENDS

Foster parents

Fill in connections where they exist.
Indicate nature of connections with a descriptive word or by drawing different kinds of
lines; _____ for strong, --------- for tenuous, ╪╪╪╪╪╪ for stressful.
Draw arrows along lines to signify flow of energy, resources etc. ➔ ➔
Identify significant people and fill in empty circles as needed.

20

At about the same time, his firm had been awarded a major contract which necessitated considerable overtime on Harold's part. He was also committed to coach a softball team and was reluctant to let the team down. The results of these shifts in Harold's relationship with his world were that Bess found herself with a major part of the child care to the point that she had given up outside activities out of her feeling that either she or Harold had to be available. Bess had tended to be quietly accommodating in the marriage but the Eco-Map made obvious to Harold what was happening to Bess and he began to think about ways he could be more helpful and supportive.

Beth had pretty much continued with her life as usual but several changes had occurred for Joyce. She had taken on a good deal of responsibility for Peter and for helping him get connected with other children, with considerable encouragement from her parents. The upshot of this had been that the children in the neighborhood had been unwelcoming and at times cruel to Peter. She had defended Peter, ended up in trouble with the neighborhood children, cut off from them, and angry with Peter.

Peter was quiet but obviously very interested and involved during the Eco-Mapping session and when asked if there was anything he wanted to add, he put his foster parents in but said he didn't see them anymore.

The Eco-Map not only provided a map of the family's relationship with its world, but also was a blueprint for change. Harold realized he would have to make more time available to the family and to Bess. Bess and Harold knew that they would have to try again to arrange for some child care. Bess also faced the fact that she had allowed herself to be cut off from many sources of gratification and that she was feeling a lot of resentment about this. Joyce had done the same kind of thing and both Joyce and Bess had to reconnect with their own lives and stop feeling so over-responsible for Peter. Harold, Bess, and the worker talked over the possibility of Peter visiting his foster home. Further, Peter's lack of social connectedness was evidenced and it was agreed that some social resources had to be developed for him so that he would not need to be so dependent on his sister.

V.   INSIDE THE FAMILY

We have looked at the family as it is immersed in its ecological environment and considered the relationships between the family and the environment as the target and the resource for change. We now turn to look at the family as a system and to consider the structure and the processes within that system as areas for understanding and potential locations for change.

The Family as a System

Before discussing specific assessment and change strategies, some initial definitions and descriptions will be clarified. First, what do we mean when we say that the family is a system? A system is a whole composed of interrelated parts. Basic to that definition is the notion that if one part of that system changes, there is a resultant impact on every other part of the system. In fact, more specifically, a family is a relatively stable, adapting, self-directing and self-regulating relationship system. In other words, the family is an intensely connected group of emotionally related people, who have existed together over time, who adapt to each other and to the world and who join together in regulating and in directing the processes within the system and processes between the system and the external world.

In understanding and attempting to help complex human systems, we have, in the past, tended to understand them as groups of individuals. Family assessments have consisted of lengthy assessments of each individual in the family together with an assessment of all the relationships between each member. This approach to understanding families leaves one faced with an overwhelming amount of data and it also leaves one unable to see the forest because of focus on the trees. Understanding each individual within a family, if it were possible, would still not take us very far in understanding the family as a system. The sum of the parts does not give us an understanding of the nature of the whole.

In the approach to understanding and helping families presented here, we will attempt to identify and to focus on some specific characteristics of family systems as a whole and we will organize our understanding and our possible targets or instruments for change in relation to these particular characteristics. We will look at two major categories of overlapping characteristics. First, we will look at family structure, at the nature of the structure, and at the way the family has organized itself. We will look at triangles, boundaries, and roles and attempt to discern stress points in the organization and ways the family can be restructured.

We will also look at the nature of family processes and consider some of those processes as potential targets for change. Among the processes, we will look at interpersonal caring which includes issues around closeness and distance and around attachment. We will look at the family self-regulatory processes and at the family's communication processes.

Although the above characteristics of family systems in no way cover the total range of family structures and processes that could be considered, these are emphasized as particularly salient areas for understanding and potentially for change.

Family Sculpture

Family members are often unaware of the nature of the family structure and cannot describe it should one ask about it. However, families make visible the structure of their relationships through their behaviors or even through the way they seat themselves in a room.

Family therapists early recognized that when a family came into a room and seated themselves, they unconsciously arranged themselves in a way that demonstrated the structure of the family's emotional system. In order to fully explore and capitalize on this way families exhibit their structure, the technique of family sculpture was devised. In this instrument for assessment and change the family is asked to nonverbally portray their relationship system through the construction of a tableau. Adoption workers have found family sculpture a useful tool in preplacement preparation of the families. Family members can negotiate in the tableau where a new member of the family might fit and how everyone will have to make an adjustment to accommodate the entrance of a new member. Sculpture can also be used in postplacement sessions to surface and make available for observation and discussion the way the structure is adapting to the presence of the child.

How to Do a Sculpture

The following basic format for family sculpture is presented as a beginning model for adoption workers who want to start using this technique. As one becomes increasingly more comfortable with the procedure, individual variations may develop out of the worker's own experience and creativity.

1. The worker begins the sculpting session by giving a simple explanation of family sculpture as a way for the family to experience and to share the current organization and patterning of the family. In postadoption services it might well be useful to tie it to the Eco-Map discussion which precedes it by describing sculpture as another way to visualize what is going on in the life of the family. It might also be useful to explain that a certain amount of change and reorganization takes place when any family has a new member, and indicate that family sculpture can offer a way for the family to see the changes that are taking place.

2. The worker then asks for a volunteer or specifically asks one family member to be the sculptor. In postadoption services it may well be most useful to ask one of the children, but not the adopted child, to do the sculpture. Not only do children enjoy doing family sculpture, but they also tend to be less defended, to be more expressive, and to involve themselves in demonstrating what is happening in the family.

3. The worker then gives the sculptor instructions on how to proceed, emphasizing that the sculpture is a nonverbal process. The primary task is to create a picture of the family by placing each member of the family in a characteristic place or position. It may be suggested that the sculptor imagine the family at home in the evenings. Where will each person be? What will they be doing? Chairs and other props may be used. Placement of the members should include not only where they are in relationship to other members but also where they are looking and how their bodies are positioned.

4. As the sculpture develops, family members may object because they see themselves in the family system in a different way. For example, if a child places dad in the corner behind the newspaper he might not like that picture of himself, nor what his son or daughter is communicating through the sculpture. It is important, however, to allow the sculptor to finish without interruption and to assure other family members that they will be able to sculpt the family later in the way they see it if they so wish.

5. The worker should give the sculptor support and help as needed, encouraging him or her to take whatever time is needed and asking enabling questions like, "Do you want mom to be looking in any particular direction?" or "Is that the way you want it? Are there any changes you want to make?"

6. After the sculptor has completed the sculpture to his or her satisfaction, and taken his or her place in the tableau, the worker assumes the role of monitor and while the actors maintain their positions asks each member how they are experiencing their place in the sculpture. This invitation surfaces disagreements on the part of the family members as to how they see the family. It surfaces how they are feeling about current family structure and may expose points of stress and tension.

As the adopted child is a new member of the family system, it is likely that his or her picture of the family might be different than the picture presented by the sculptor. In postadoption services it might be a good idea to invite an adopted child at this point to sculpt the family the way he or she sees it. Such a sculpture may well express how the adopted child is feeling and experiencing the entry into the family. He or she may place himself or herself next to the one member of the family with whom he or she feels the most comfortable. He or she may place himself or herself rather uncertainly on the borders of the family, relatively distant from most members. However the child does it, the sculpture communicates to the family members how the adopted child sees their system and his or her place in it.

The Use of Family Sculpture in Postadoptive Services

Family sculpture is a powerful projective technique. The very fact that it is nonverbal means that the exercise taps into and makes available the emotional system. Practitioners may object that a family sculpture session will bring too much to the surface, that the difficulty of the family and the adoptive child in developing this new family structure will be too dramatically portrayed and will be too upsetting for the adopted child. However, it can be assumed that the child is already feeling and is deeply aware of everything that is being expressed in this sculpture, and is feeling it every day. The family system structure is usually covert but it is present in everything the family does. It is easier to surface something, deal with it, and talk about it than for the adopted child to carry the burden of experiencing tension and stress in a family system that is being denied. The whole family can experience the sculpture together, they can talk about it and the worker is there to help them to understand and to normalize the experience. The worker can be very reassuring in saying, "But this is what families always go through when they try to change, there are always periods of adaptation." The worker can assure the family and the adopted child that the stress and tension experienced is a part of the transition to a new family structure and the important thing is that everybody can see it and deal with it. Perhaps the family can even make changes in it.

A variety of issues may become apparent while doing the family sculpture. One of the major sources of tension in families with children, and it is primarily in such families with whom sculpture would be used, is around sibling issues. Competitive feelings about where the adopted child is positioned between the siblings and the parents quickly emerge. How close is the adopted child to either one of the parents? Is the child located between the parents or between one of the siblings and the parents? Is one of the siblings whose position was very close to the mother now separated from the mother by the adopted child? The whole reorganization of the parent-child system becomes visible through the sculpture, and the tension that understandably exists will become apparent. Systems have difficulty with change. That does not mean they cannot change or that members of the system do not want to change. Nevertheless, change creates discomfort and this discomfort can be commented upon and accepted.

It may well be that children in the family are feeling guilty and anxious about the rivalry that is surfaced. They have participated in the decision to adopt and were excited about it, but when the adopted child became a reality, they found that they had to share the household with this other person full-time and it wasn't as much fun as they thought it was going to be. The feelings of rivalry exist and are real and cannot be ignored. However, the feelings of guilt around the feelings of rivalry can be targets for change. Universalizing and accepting those feelings of rivalry can help diminish the guilt. Further, intense feelings of rivalry may indicate that the adoptive parents have leaned over backwards in their attempt to include the adopted child, insufficiently attending to the feelings of displacement experienced by their biological or previously adopted children. They may worry that, if they do something special or spend time alone or in other ways attend to the individual needs of another child in the family, the adopted child will feel left out.

The sculpture will also portray the extent to which the child has been integrated into the family system. Is he or she located on the periphery of the family or is the child placed well within the system? Or, is there uncertainty about where the child seems to belong, uncertainty that is expressed by the child and the family members changing the structure several times? Another area that may surface is around the nature of personal boundaries, and of differences that may exist between the adoptive family's sense of what is an appropriate distance-closeness ratio, of what is too close or too far away, and how the child relates to boundaries. One family will sculpt itself with considerable closeness, with family members touching or even with their arms around each other, while others from different families with a different sense of family boundaries would feel suffocated in such a family, stating, "I couldn't stand being that close in a family." On the other hand, should someone sculpt their family demonstrating a fair amount of distance between each member, an observer coming from a family that has a different sense of what is appropriately close could experience the sculpture as a picture of loneliness and alienation. One of the points of tension that exist between adopted children and their families is a different view about personal boundaries. The different view is not only an expression of the fact that the adopted child has experienced in the past a different system with different notions about boundaries, but also, as was discussed in our explorations of issues of attachment, the child is not ready for an adult to come as close as the adoptive parents wish to do. The adopted child may well experience the kind of closeness that feels comfortable in the adoptive family as intrusive and frightening and may need to preserve more distance between him- or herself and the family and a firmer boundary around his or her rather shaky sense of identity. The adopted child will express this issue around boundaries during the sculpture, either through his own sculpture or an alteration he wishes to make in the way another member of the family sculpts the system.

Another characteristic of the family sculpture that may well surface in the sculpture is a picture of the major triangles in the family system. Murray Bowen has written that the triangle is the basic building block of all interpersonal systems.[11] He writes that a two-person system is basically unstable and that in periods of stress and tension a third member tends to be brought in to deal with, to detour, or become the receptacle of that tension. Two people may triangulate a third by finding closeness through talking about the third person. The third member of the triangle is frequently attempting to become a member of the close twosome and to push another member of the twosome out. Sibling rivalry over attentions from parents is an example of that dynamic. This is well illustrated when a younger child in a family provokes an older child to become aggressive or threatening and then runs to a parent for comfort. The parents, if they get trapped by the triangulating move, will punish the older child and comfort the younger. This establishes the triangle as consisting of parent and younger child on the inside and the older child on the outside.

Uncomfortable triangles may also exist among members of the sibling system. For example, if there were two children in the family before the adopted child was placed, a natural triangle is set up. The triangle among siblings can be seen as two children close in the triangle and the third trying to get in. The situation may often vary where children take turns about who is close and who is on the outside. Such uncomfortable triangles in the family system become apparent in the sculpture and may provide another guideline for interventive help. An uncomfortable triangle is resolved in a very simple way and that is by converting it into three close and communicating twosomes.

The Family Sculpture as a Blueprint for Change

One of the advantages of family sculpture is that the process can be ongoing throughout the family meetings. It is not static and an experienced worker can begin to use it not only as an assessment tool but to help the family make use of it as a blueprint for a change. Following the initial sculpture, it may be possible to ask any member of the family, including the adopted child, how they would like the sculpture to be. This involves the family members in enacting and experiencing possible solutions to current issues of stress and conflict. A very interesting and useful experience can develop when all of the family begin to work together without words on how they would like it to be simply by repositioning themselves and others. There will be some conflict and there will be some juggling and negotiation. Two of the children may begin pushing each other to get into a particular spot in the family system. But in time, the family may be able to get to a place that is comfortable for each member of the family. Such a family structure can be considered a blueprint for change, and interventive strategies can be developed to consolidate or make permanent this change. Even enacting, experiencing and sharing the changed structure through the sculpting session is a powerful instrument of change, and may in fact be enough to bring about the altering of the structure to a more comfortable balance.

Systemic Interviewing with Families

Although family sculpture is the fastest and in many ways the easiest way to objectify the family structure and make it available for study and for change, other assessments and interviewing techniques can also bring forth this picture. First, the worker can observe the behavior of the family in the session, the way they arrange themselves, and the way they relate to one another, without actually asking the family to do a sculpture.

Family interviewing, of course, is a major way of uncovering the family structure, and also, if carefully done, can more effectively surface the directing, regulating, and communicating processes that are going on within the family.

Systemic family interviewing, however, is a special kind of interviewing. It is not multiple individual interviewing. It focuses not on the feelings and interpretations of the individual members but on the relationships among members and the transactional events within the family. The family therapist, Mara Palazzoli, and her colleagues in Milan, Italy, have spelled out a useful and a specific approach to systemic interviewing with families as follows.[12]

Hypothesizing

In order not to become lost in the system and in the overwhelming amount of data available, it is useful before an interview with a family for the worker to develop a hypothesis or a "hunch" about what is going on in the family. This hypothesis can then be either proved or disproved through questioning in the family meeting. Developing such a hypothesis gives the worker some direction in interviewing, so that he or she does not get led by the family off the track and into the areas that may not be salient to the current situation. The hypothesis is developed out of whatever knowledge is already known by the worker prior to the session. In the case of postadoption services, a tremendous amount of information is known and the worker, prior to seeing the family, should think through that information and develop some hunches about what may be going on in that system.

Following the development of a hypothesis, the course of the interview with the family will then be directed toward exploring factual information that can either support the hypothesis or disprove it and lead to the development of a new hypothesis.

Examples of hypotheses are as varied as are families. In postadoption services, initial hypotheses may grow out of an understanding of the common themes or issues in placement. For example, when the worker learns that the adoptive child is acting out in some pretty destructive ways, it is likely that the child is testing, that he or she is beginning to attach and is frightened. Another common hypothesis would be that the family is experiencing tension and conflict as old relationship patterns have been disturbed by the new family member's arrival. In other situations, it could be possible that the parents are feeling tentative in their roles, that they do not feel entitled to take on the parental authority and are communicating uncertain or conflicting messages to the child. Reports of sibling fights suggest rivalry and some difficulty in the sibling subsystem about roles, status with parents, and/or hierarchy.

Hypotheses, of course, are tentative and are developed in order to give direction to the inquiry and, as Palazzoli points out, a disproven hypothesis also contributes considerable information and leads to the formulation of a new hypothesis.

Systemic Questions

Palazzoli and other family therapists have identified several major types or kinds of questions that yield information about the family system as a system and the processes going on within that system. The first type of questions may be called "tracking" questions. These questions are based on the assumption that in some way or for some reason, the family's response to a behavior is maintaining that behavior.[13] In fact, it is often discovered that the family member's solution to the problematic behavior is inadvertently exacerbating the very behavior they wish to interrupt. If strategies can alter the reinforcing familial response, the behavior is likely to diminish.

Tracking questions follow and identify the sequence of transactions around the problematic behavior and may identify how the behavior is maintained and what can be done about it.

For example, Johnny, age 5, the adopted child, who has been with his adoptive family for three months, has tantrums. Instead of the tantrum being seen and understood as an isolated internal process going on within Johnny, the worker's effort is to understand what it is in the transactions of the family that although not initially creating the tantrums, now, in some way, continues them. Also we want to know what the outcomes of the tantrum are for the relationship system. The following segment of a family interview illustrates tracking.

Worker: When Johnny begins to have a tantrum, who is the first person to do something?

Mother: I am, usually.

Worker: And what do you do?

Mother: I usually talk to him and try to get him to calm down.

Worker: And then what happens?

Mother: Nothing! I mean he continues to kick and scream.

Worker: Then who does what?

Mother: Then George (father) usually comes running.

Worker: And then what do you do, George?

Father: Well, I usually tell Florence to leave him alone, that he'll quiet--but she won't do that.

Worker: George, what are you thinking at the time about the way Florence is dealing with the tantrum?

Father: I don't think she should try to talk him out of it. I think she should just put him in his room.

Mother: How can I put him anywhere?

Bill (10-year-old brother): Yeah. They start arguing about what to do!

Worker: And where are you at this point, Bill?

Bill: I usually am around.

Worker: And what do you do when your parents start to argue about how to handle the tantrum?

And so the tracking questions continue until the whole complex sequence of interactions of which the tantrum is a part is clear.

A very useful kind of question relates behavior to the passage of time. For example, if father makes the statement that "Bill is lazy," one can respond by inquiring whether he was before or after a particular event occurred. For instance, was he lazier before he started school or after he started school? If one learns that he was lazier after he started school, then find out was he lazier before second grade or after second grade. Such questions begin to narrow down when the laziness seems to have begun and how the laziness relates to other events in the family. Again, it shifts the consideration of a personal attribute to a discussion of relationships between people and events. In postadoption services, before-and-after questions are very important as the family is reacting to a major event, the addition of the child to the family. Sometimes certain behaviors in the system will emerge as having begun or become more frequent after the placement. At other times, however, problems which people assume to be connected with adoption, after careful interviewing, will be discovered to be transactions that preceded the placement of the child in the home, or seem to be related to another event.

Finally, a very useful form of inquiry is a hypothetical question. In this kind of question, the interviewer presents a hypothetical event or happening to the family and then inquires about the family members' possible responses. For example, "If mom were sick and had to stay home for a whole week, who in the family would stay home and take care of her? Who would cheer her up? Who would be the most worried?" Quite quickly, considerable information about roles in the family has come to light. Hypothetical questions can be combined with rating questions, for example, in interviewing in postadoption services--"If Mary (8-year-old adopted child) got very very sad one day, who would cheer her up the most? Who next? Who next?" or "If Mary had a very important secret, who would she be most likely to tell it to? Who next? Who next? Who last?"

Clearly, these are closeness/distance questions which surface the same kind of structural information about the family relationship systems as does family sculpture.

A second kind of question that surfaces a good deal about the relationship system Palazzoli terms "gossip in presence." By "gossiping in the presence" is meant that questions are asked of members of the family about relationships between other members of the family, but only if they are present. For example, it might be possible to ask brother Peter, age 12, what he thinks about what is going on between Bobby, the adopted child, and his 7-year-old sister. Then one might ask the mother to talk about what she thinks about what Peter has just said about Bobby and his sister. After getting Peter to respond to what his mother said about his views, one can then turn to father and ask him what he thinks about Bobby and his sister's relationship. This circular "gossiping in presence" can keep going around the family.

Another kind of question rates the extent to which each family member exhibits a particular characteristic. Rating questions are particularly useful when a statement of attribution is made, for example, as illustrated in the following sequence.

Mother: Alan (the adopted child) has a terrible temper--a very low boiling point!

Worker: Who has the lowest boiling point in the family?

Dick (age 13--jumps in): Dad. He has the lowest.

Worker (to mother): What do you think about that?

Mother: No, I think Alan's is lower than Dick's. Then comes Ralph (the father).

Worker: Who next?

Mother: Let me see. Then Dick, then Janet and last me.

Worker: So the women have higher boiling points than the men! Now it's your turn, Dick, how would you rate boiling points?

Dick: First Dad, then Alan, then mom, then me, and last Janet.

And so the rating continues. Not only is considerable information gained but a negative characteristic that was being attributed to one family member (in this case the adopted child) becomes a characteristic that is, at least to some extent, shared by everyone in the family.

Diagramming Families

Whether information about the family structure comes through doing a family sculpture or through systemic interviewing techniques, it is important that the worker be able to visualize the family structure as a system. It is very difficult to capture the complexity of a relationship system in words--not unlike the task of describing a football game over the radio. Paper-and-pencil simulations can diagram the family structure so that the worker may be able to picture it, study it, and think about how it might be altered.

The family structure can be diagrammed in many ways. The following is a system which has been found to be useful by the author and which employs some of the symbols used in the Eco-Map.

The space on paper is used as a metaphor for emotional distance and closeness, as space is in sculpture. A female is depicted by a circle, a male by a box. Conflict is a line with hash marks. Attention or investment can be depicted by arrows and cut offs or alienation by an opaque boundary line. A tenuous connection can be a dotted line and a strong one a thick line or several lines together.

The best way to draw a family diagram is to imagine or develop a mental image of how the family would be likely to sculpt itself and then to transfer that image onto paper.

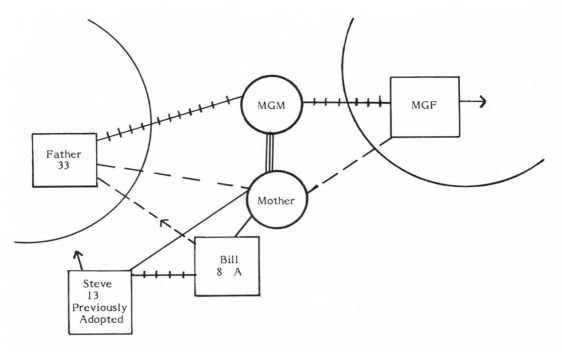

This is a map of a three-generational family system. Bill was placed with the family four months previously. He has some health and some school problems and mother has become extremely involved with him. Mother is also very involved with her mother, talking to her or seeing her daily. Her father is quite distant and her parents have had chronic marital difficulties. Father is also distant, very involved in his job. Steve has been in the home since age 4. He had been very close to mother but for the past two years has been attempting to move away from her and would like to be more involved with father. Steve and Bill have been experiencing some conflict as Steve feels two ways about being on the outside of the newly formed triangle consisting of Mother and Bill as a close twosome with him on the outside. Father is also clearly on the outside and it is possible that he has always felt rather on the outside of two triangles, one where his wife and mother-in-law formed the close twosome and one where his wife and first Steve and then Bill are in the close position.

It takes many words to even begin to describe the complex network of relationships which can be so quickly portrayed in a family diagram.

Helping Families to Restructure

Adoption is a restructuring process, that is, the entry of the new member into the family has altered the family structure and brought about change for every member in the family system. During the postadoption period, the family may experience discomfort or conflict around the restructuring process. One of the ways to help a family in postadoption services is to help them make some shifts in the way they have organized since the placement.

We have already discussed some restructuring moves when interventions related to enhancing or altering the family's relationship with its ecological environment are described. For example, suggesting that the mother become more active outside the home, for her to take up an abandoned activity, to visit friends, or to make some babysitting arrangements are basically restructuring moves as they alter her position in the system. Also, encouraging the father to take on a specific role that has been carried by the mother to enable her to go out also restructures the family. Not only does it move the mother temporarily out of the system but it also serves to strengthen the father's relationship with the children.

Restructuring interventions and other efforts to bring about change generally consist of either events or transactions or new understandings that occur within the family meeting or changes that are enacted outside of the meeting in the form of assignments or directives given by the worker.

For example, going through a family sculpture in the family meeting and processing it can be a powerful change strategy within the family meetings as the members of the family experience the family's structure and also experience patterning the system in a different way. "Homework" assignments which encourage the family to enact the structural changes in their daily lives enhance the change process.

Before discussing some examples of change efforts, it may be useful to describe the general change method of giving assignments or directives.

When giving an assignment or a directive, the worker gives very explicit instructions to the family concerning something they want the members to do at or within a specified period of time. There are many kinds of assignments that may be given but they should meet certain requirements. First, they should be clearly and precisely stated and should describe something family members are to do. Second, they should be given to the family quite firmly, not tentatively suggested. Third, everyone in the family should be mentioned in the assignment even if the way they are mentioned is to be told to do nothing. Finally, the family should be asked to repeat to the worker what the assignment is to make sure they are clear.

Assignments must be distinguished from "advice giving." An assignment is not telling the family a better way to do things, it is asking the family members to enact or to practice a structural change in the family system. The following are some examples of efforts to restructure families and assignments which may be a part of the effort.

A major kind of assignment is geared to enhancing an alliance between two members of the family. When triangles were discussed earlier, it was stated that the best way to handle the triangle is to turn it into three strong, communicating dyads. In a family where there is a central triangle with one person on the outside and two people in the inside positions, assignments may be for each of the three dyads in the triangle to spend some time together as twosomes and get involved in a particular pleasurable activity. Strengthening these dyadic alliances minimizes the triangulation and diminishes conflict.

In one home, an 8-year-old boy had been adopted and the family's 12-year-old boy, although participating in the adoption, was having some difficulty with the loss of his role as an only child. Before the adopted child had come, the father and the son had regular camping trips alone together. These were very important events in the life of the boy, and the father had promised him that they could still go camping together. In talking with the family it was learned that the father and the two boys were going off on a camping trip together. This trip had been planned for the following week and although the father and the adopted son were planning this with great eagerness, the older boy appeared to be rather sullen and angry. The worker developed a hypothesis that the shift toward including the adopted son in the father-son subsystem was very important. However, this could not be done to the exclusion of dyadic relationship between the father and the older son. She gave an assignment prescribing that the father and the older son take a short trip alone together, something that they planned and something that made particular sense for a 12-year-old, but that would be less appropriate for an 8-year-old. Because when assignments are given they should include everyone in the family, an assignment was also given to the mother to take the adopted son to visit her brother at the same time, which was something she wanted to do.

Frequently, the major alliance that needs to be strengthened is between the marital pair. It is not necessarily that the marital pair has been having difficulty, but it may well have happened that with the placement of the child in the home, the parents have had less time for one another. A very common assignment is to prescribe that the parents plan regular evenings or even a weekend away alone together. Many adoptive parents tend to focus too much on their parenting, and sometimes need permission to take care of their own needs, as well as the needs of their other children. In their anxiety to do the right thing, they may tend to be overinvolved and overconcerned about the adopted child. Such overconcern can heighten the adopted child's anxiety around succeeding, and assignments which encourage an adoptive family to attend to each other's needs and to be less intensely absorbed in the task of integrating this new member into the family system may be useful.

Another characteristic of the system which often requires some alteration and adaptation is the family's boundaries. Attention may need to be given to boundaries between individuals, between subsystems, or to the external boundary around the family.

Boundaries between individuals may be strengthened by interventions made by the worker in the family meetings or through assignments. In the session, it is important to make sure that everyone speaks for themselves and that no one explains or interprets what another is thinking. As Minuchin tends to comment to families "people should tell their own story and own their own memories."[14] Assignments can also strengthen interpersonal boundaries. For example, the adopted child's possessions and room are metaphors for the self. The door to the room and the adoptive mother's access are metaphors for the boundary between mother and child. Frequently, assignments can be made around the child's room and possessions, which can define the interpersonal boundary and lessen behavior on the parent's part that can be experienced as intrusiveness by the child.

Intergenerational boundaries may also need clarifying. For example, the children in the family are probably exhibiting a fair amount of tension and fighting as they integrate the new member into the household. Parents are frequently drawn into this, both forming a triangle and also violating an intergenerational boundary. That is, the parents are getting into the children's business, because sibling fights are clearly the business of the sibling system. The parents' entry into those battles serves to escalate them. An assignment could be for the adoptive parents to stay out of the children's battles but at the same time, an assignment would have to be given to the youngsters in the family concerning devising a way to problem-solve. For example, it is possible to give the child who seems to be the most frequent instigator of the battles the task of recording the battles that take place between the other siblings and bringing a record of those battles into the next meeting with the family. This clarifies that the children's battles are their business but also dramatically alters the role of the major instigator. It makes it almost impossible for him or her to start a fight because it is very hard to act and to record at the same time. The recorder assignment immediately puts the person in a position of observer rather than participant.

Another kind of assignment attempts to alter the processes around discipline and the confusion over who is handling what. For example, in the discussion above, about the little boy who had the tantrum, specific assignments should be given on how to handle the tantrum in the future. This assignment should be related to what appears to be the reinforcing outcome of the tantrum, and should alter the outcome. For example, if every time the child has a tantrum, the whole family congregates around him or her and the child is the center of attention and the center of considerable argument and conflict among the family members who are trying to figure out what to do, it would appear that it would make sense to assign one person to be in charge of handling the tantrum. An often-used family assignment is that on odd days the father is in charge of handling problematic behavior and on even days the mother is, while on the seventh day they both are. Such an assignment tends to be used when there is considerable conflict between the parents on how to handle a particular behavior.

External Boundaries, Entitlement, and Rituals

Rituals are a powerful and universally utilized way of enacting, experiencing, and integrating change. Marriages, Bar Mitzvahs, funerals, and graduations all mark developmental changes and/or changes in family structure. Rituals have been used extensively by family therapists as instruments of change.[15] They may be brief sequences of behaviors that are repeated regularly at specified times, similar to lighting the candles on the Sabbath or a more elaborate one-time event. One-time public rituals have many functions and organize social recognition and support around an important change.

Many adoptive families have recognized the need for some kind of ritual which enacts the adoption by the family of a child and have expressed disappointment when the final hearing before the court was hurried and without ceremony. Some families, perhaps not intentionally, have used other kinds of rituals as a stand-in for an adoption ritual, for example, a baptism or a christening. In reality, however, such rituals pertain to the child's relationship to the church, not to the family.

Entitlement and belonging and the social support and sanctioning of the adoption can be strengthened and enhanced through the use of an adoption ritual which announces the child's membership in the family, and enacts and celebrates this important event. The adoption ceremony can vary from family to family, depending on the style and preferences of the family and the age of the child.

To be powerful, however, it should be ceremonial, serious, and publicly witnessed. Hopefully, the ceremony would be followed by some sort of party or reception. Some words should be spoken by all those involved, not only by the parents, and if old enough, the child, but also by the other children and perhaps other important extended family members. It would also be important for former foster parents and any biological kin with whom contact can be maintained to be included. As no recognized form exists, it is the family's task to plan the ceremony and to decide on the words to be spoken. Similar to a marriage, the words should describe the event which is taking place and the obligations and privileges which accrue to the changing status.

The timing of the adoption ceremony should be geared, not necessarily to the final formalization of the adoption, which may be experienced by the family and child as too long after the actual placement, but should be held when the family feels ready to do so.

The adoption ritual validates the child's membership in the family. It alters the exterior family boundary by opening it to include this new member but also through strengthening family cohesiveness. The enactment of this claiming ritual enhances a sense of entitlement on the part of family and child and involves the extended family and friendship network in this important family event.

Enhancing Communication

An important strategy for helping families is the enhancement of communication among all the members. It is difficult for families to problem-solve, to change their structure, to deal with the impact of changes on family members if the members are unable to give or hear feedback or to tell each other what they think and how they feel.

The family meetings and the various change strategies described above will all demand or create enhanced communication. Family sculpture helps families show each other where they are and how they feel and vitalizes the communication system. Many of the restructuring assignments rely on increased communication among members of the family. The adoption ritual is a dramatic communication to the child and to the world that the child is now and henceforth a member of this family.

There are some special problems in communication that are particularly associated with adoption that may well require special help. First is the fact that the child and the family talk a different language.

Families share meanings that have developed over time. They know what they mean when they speak to one another and they understand gestures and looks. They also communicate with many private references to the past and to shared experiences over time. A new child coming into the home must be inducted into this communication system. Family members are often unaware of how private their discourse is. They may be impatient when an adopted child doesn't seem to understand the family communication and a major intervention in working with such a family is to help them talk together. Communication must be clarified and the worker can help family members let each other know when they don't understand what is being said and to help family members accept and respond to the fact that someone new to the system often does not understand the communication. In working with an adoptive family, communication skills can be practiced in family meetings where the worker models clarifying communication by expressing her own uncertainty about the meaning of the communication. His or her position may not be dissimilar to that of the adopted child as both are somewhat outside the system.

A second fact that interferes with communication in an adoptive family is that the adopted child has a life that until very recently has been lived separately from the adoptive family. His or her associations and memories are not shared with the family and if the family transmits the message that the past is not to be shared or commented upon, the child will learn to keep his or her own counsel and there will be a sharp break in the communication between child and family. The child should be encouraged to communicate, to reminisce, to comment on simple things like "I have been here before," when a familiar place is revisited, or "My foster mother used to help me with my homework, but she had a lot of trouble with math." It is useful for the adoptive family to ask about previous experiences to indicate to the adopted child that it is all right to bring up these memories and to include them in the family conversation.

If the family is having trouble accepting the difference between adoption and biological family building, they will subtly and even unconsciously let the child know that communication about events or people before the adoption took place makes them uncomfortable. The child will quickly respond to this by ceasing to share memories and a real discontinuity will begin to exist for the child. On the other hand, if the family shows a genuine interest in the child's life and if the child is able to share, he or she will be helped to integrate past, present, and future. Visits to former foster parents and the maintenance of connections with biological kin will also keep communication open, help the family to share the life of the child, and maintain the child's continuous sense of self.

The Life Book is a very useful aid to sharing and communicating as well as a vital support to the child's effort to maintain his or her identity. Widely used in adoption, the Life Book is a scrapbook which contains facts, pictures, and mementos of the child's life. Agency workers have often done Life Books with children prior to adoption. These books can be shared by the child and the family. If a Life Book has not been done, it would be useful for the adoptive parents and the worker to work together on this project. It is also important for the child to share the family's "Life Books," family albums, slides, movies, scrapbooks and other mementos. This acquaints the child with the family's past and helps with the process of socializing the child into the family.

Reframing and Paradoxical Interventions

As social workers in adoption agencies become more experienced in work with families in postadoption services, other interventive methods developed by family therapists can be adopted for work with these families.[16]

Strategic interventions, for example, are aimed at altering or interrupting the stabilizing or homeostatic processes within the family. They may challenge the family's way of looking at and explaining behavior or events. Strategic approaches also surface the positive or maintenance functions that are being served by problematic behavior and interrupt that homeostatic cycle.

Although an extensive discussion of strategic interventions can not be undertaken here, some examples may serve to illustrate the potential of these methods and stimulate workers who are deeply involved in delivering postadoption services to seek opportunities to become further acquainted with strategic approaches.

Reframing[17] is a change strategy which challenges the family's view or interpretation of a particular behavior or event. It alters the meaning the behavior has to the family and thus alters responses to the behavior. Reframing changes the framework of meaning in which an event or a behavior is embedded.

For example, Tommy, an adopted 7-year-old, began to exhibit hostile and angry behaviors which were threatening to drive the family away. The worker hypothesized that the abrupt change in Tommy's behavior was related to the fact that he was beginning to form some positive feelings for the new family and that those feelings were stimulating anxiety about abandonment and loss and reawakening old pain and old longings. The adoptive parents, however, were understanding the behavior as meaning that Tommy hated them and they were responding with hurt, helplessness, and anger.

The worker reframed by saying "Tommy must be beginning to care for you a great deal or he wouldn't be so frightened." If the reframing works, and it often does, from then on, Tommy's angry behavior is understood by the family as a signal of this growing attachment. This, naturally, alters their responses.

Paradoxical interventions have been used with success in situations where adopted children, anticipating rejection, provoke it by their behavior.[18] There are many different paradoxical strategies, but a major one is to identify the function of problematic behavior and encourage its continuance on the basis of what might happen if the behavior should cease. For example, in a family meeting, it is possible to say to an older child who is provoking rejection, "I think you should think of something bad enough to do so the the family will have to send you back--then you won't have to keep waiting for it to happen. What do you think might finally do it?"

If the behavior improves following the paradoxical intervention, the worker could follow it up with, "I am worried that things are changing too fast and that Janie is being too good! Janie, how can you really be sure they are going to keep you if you don't give them a good reason to send you back?"

Such comments may sound nonsensical and family members may laugh or become annoyed. They are not nonsense, however, but really lay bare the central meaning of the interactions.

Paradoxical interventions are particularly useful where people are stuck in repetitive destructive sequences of behavior and where there is strong resistance to and fear about change.

Strategic interventions require a careful assessment because their power depends on their accuracy. However, if they can interrupt stuck negative transactions and shorten the painful testing period that must be survived if an adoption is to work, they should be considered as possible avenues to change.

VI. THE FAMILY THROUGH TIME:
FAMILIES OF ORIGIN

We have looked at the family in its world and considered ways of enhancing the family's relationship with its ecological environment through postadoption services. We have looked inside the family and suggested ways of intervening to alter some aspect of the structure or the process of that system.

We will now turn to look at families as intergenerational systems that have developed through time and at the implications of that view for adoption services. We will consider the importance of the child's family of origin in his life adjustment as well as the potential impact of the adoptive family history on the current situation. This emphasis on the use of family history in understanding the life of the individual and the family grows from the conviction that the main source of each person's sense of self and personal identity is to be found in the saga of his or her family.

The starting point of this approach is an assumption that all people are deeply immersed in their family systems. The family affects people's perceptions of who they are, how they think and communicate, and how they see themselves and others. It influences what they choose to do and be, whom they choose to be with and to love and marry, and how they choose to structure their new family.

Perhaps this perspective can best be illustrated through an example. Recently, I was meeting with an adoptive family around some serious postadoption adjustment issues. The tension was high and there was a real possibility that Steve, a ten-year-old who had been placed in the home four months earlier, was not going to be able to stay. He was acting violently and abusively and the parents were questioning whether they were going to be able to continue to tolerate his behavior but felt helpless in dealing with it. Their daughter, Janet, age twelve, who had been adopted a few years earlier, was also reacting to the stress and tension by returning to the withdrawn behavior she had shown the first year after she had been placed. The system was clearly in crisis and seemed stuck in destructive and repetitive interactions.

As we struggled with the complex issues involved in building this family, I suddenly had the sense that also in the room, powerfully affecting the structure and the processes developing in this nuclear family, were the shadows of the four families of origin of these four biologically unrelated people. Family therapist Murray Bowen has said, "When I see an individual, I never see him alone. I see the generations of his family standing behind him,"[19] and so it was that the room was crowded with the images of four families that were having such influence on this family system. I knew if we understood more about these families, if each member of this new family was aware of and could deal with what they were bringing from their families of origin, we would have come a long way toward working out the current family issues.

I shared my vision of the crowded room with the family and it was decided that everyone would tell about their families. The parents went first, and although initially reluctant, they did share a good deal, negatives as well as positives. This enabled the children to talk about their families, something neither had ever done.

Much vital information was exchanged that clarified some of the intense interactions which were taking place within the family. Just a few of the many important themes that emerged will be mentioned here. Father, in telling about his family, admitted that he had been abused as a child. This was one reason why his heart had gone out to Steve, the newly adopted youngster, who had been abused by his biological father and subsequently in one of his foster homes. Steve's violent, abusive, and destructive temper flare-ups left the adoptive mother in tears and father overwhelmed with impotent rage while Steve was full of remorse and fear. Steve was amazed to learn of his adoptive father's childhood and began to really listen when he told him that he knew he overreacted and was not handling things well but Steve's violence brought those painful memories back. Larry, the father, had vowed he would never raise his hand to a child as his father had, but was able, in his rage, to consider no other option. This left him feeling helpless, exactly like he had felt as a child.

This sharing had many outcomes, one of which was that Steve, who had felt so different and "bad" began to learn that he was not the only one who had troubles. Mother shared the fact that her grandfather had been an alcoholic and although she was his favorite and she felt especially close to him, his behavior was unpredictable. She never knew what to expect with him. She was experiencing some of the same uncertainty with Steve. Even more importantly, mother shared the fact that she had had a brother, three years younger than she, who had been killed in a farming accident when she was eleven. The loss of this only son was a devastating blow for her parents and for her and somehow things had never been the same again. Steve was in some respects a replacement for her brother and the threatened failure of the adoption reactivated that old loss and the accompanying feelings of grief and guilt.

Janet responded to learning about her mother's lost brother by, for the first time, talking about her own younger brother who had been placed in another adoptive home before Janet was placed. Steve's presence in the home had reactivated that old loss as well as stimulating loyalty conflicts. How could she connect with a new brother when she remained deeply--and secretly--attached to her biological brother? One concrete outcome of this sharing was that, in time, arrangements were made for visiting between Janet and her brother.

This led to Steve very tentatively mentioning his grandmother, to whom he had been very attached. Grandmother had provided a lot of care as Steve's mother, a heroin addict who had died two years previously, had been neglectful and frequently had left Steve with his grandmother. Although it took time and careful planning on the worker's part and although it was initially frightening for the adoptive parents, arrangements were made for Steve to be able to maintain contact with his grandmother. Mother's important attachment to her grandfather helped her to support Steve in maintaining this important connection.

The exploration of family histories has been used in family assessment and preparation for adoption, surfacing the meaning of the wish to adopt and clarifying the expectations and role assignments of a child who steps into a particular spot in the family tree.

In postadoption services, understanding and sharing the family histories of all the members of the family sets current transactions in perspective, clarifies their meaning and may point to ways to bring about change.

Constructing a Genogram

As the Eco-Map charts the family's relationships with its world, the genogram is a paper-and-pencil simulation which charts the intergenerational family and is a useful way of gathering and organizing family history.[20] The genogram is a family tree or a map of three or more generations of a family that records genealogical relationships, major family events, occupations, losses, family migrations and dispersal, identifications and role assignments, and information about alignment and communication patterns.

It is best to approach drawing a genogram with a large piece of paper. It is important that the genogram be uncrowded and clear so visual examination is possible. Plain white pads, the size of desk blotters, with card-board backing, available in office supply stores, are useful and convenient for this task.

The skeleton of the genogram tends to follow the conventions of genetic and genealogical charts. As in the Eco-Map, male is indicated by a square; female by a circle; and if the sex of a person is unknown, by a triangle. The triangle tends to be used when a person says, "I think there were seven children in my grandfather's family, but I have no idea whether they were males or females," or, "My mother lost a full-term child five years before I was born, but I don't know what sex it was."

A marital pair is indicated by a connecting line, and it is useful to add the marriage date, 5-10-1966. Offspring are shown as follows:

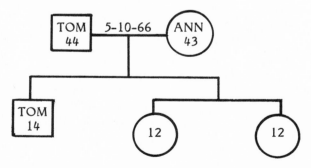

They are generally lined up according to age, starting with the oldest on the left. The above family has an older son followed by a set of twins.

A divorce is generally portrayed by a broken line, and again, it is useful to include dates.

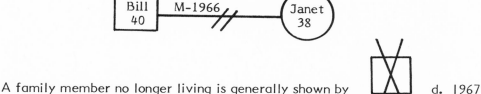

A family member no longer living is generally shown by [diagram] d. 1967

Thus, a complex, but not untypical, reconstituted family may be drawn as follows:

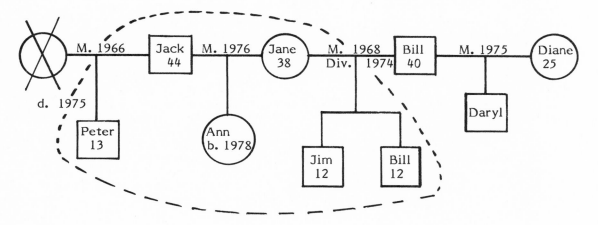

It is useful to draw a dotted line around the family members who compose the household. Incidentally, such a family chart enables the worker to quickly grasp "who's who" in complicated reconstituted families.

With these basic building blocks expanded horizontally to depict the contemporary generation of siblings and cousins and vertically to chart the generations through time, it is possible to chart any family, given sufficient paper, patience, and information.

As one charts the skeletal structure of the family, it is also important to fill this out with the rich and varied data which portray the saga of the family. Many different kinds of information can be important and it is often hard to know in advance what kinds of material will be salient.

Given names, both first and middle, should be added to the genogram. This information identifies family members, indicates naming patterns, and surfaces identifications. How has the naming of the adopted child been handled in this family? Although parents should generally be discouraged from changing the first name of any child beyond infancy, often a new middle name is given. Where did the name come from? Was it the name of an important family member? Who else in the family is named after a relative?

Dates of birth and dates of death record when members joined the family, their longevity, and family losses. Birth dates indicate the age of the family members when important events occurred. They indicate how early or late in a marriage a child came and the age of the parents at the birth. In a sense, birth, marriage, and death dates mark the movement of the family through time.

It is particularly important to note family losses and consider the possible implication of those losses for the family-building process. The replacement phenomenon, the tendency of families and of individuals to replace important lost people with other family members, is widespread. The possibility that Steve was an emotional replacement for his adoptive mother's lost brother emerged in the situation reported above.

Birth dates also identify each individual's place in the sibship. This brings to the surface such potential roles as "older responsible," "firstborn son," or "baby." It is also relevant to discover who else in the family has occupied the same sibling position. Sibling positions can be a powerful source of intergenerational identifications.

Steve occupied the same place in the new family's sibship as did both the adoptive mother's and Janet's lost brothers. This had important implications for how they each responded to him.

Place of birth and current place of residence mark the movement of the family through space. Such information charts the family's patterns of dispersal, surfacing major immigrations or migrations, and brings attention to periods of loss, change, and upheaval. On the other hand, such information may point to the fact that generations of a family have stayed within a fairly small geographical radius.

Picturing the family's movement through space may communicate a good deal about family boundaries and norms concerning mobility. Is this a family that "holds on" or "lets go"? Locating family members in space also begins to tap the extent to which the family continues to be intimately connected with extended family members. Is the extended family available and interested? What is their attitude toward the applicants' wish to adopt?

Occupations of family members acquaint one with the interests and talents, the successes and failures, and the varied socioeconomic statuses that are found in most families. Occupational patterns may also point to intrafamily identifications, and often portray family prescriptions and expectations. These prescriptions and expectations are very important to understand in discussions with families.

For example, if family occupations cover a wide range of blue- and white-collar positions and if some of the admired and valued members are in blue-collar occupations, it may well indicate that a family can tolerate differences in interests and in educational level or achievement. This kind of acceptance of difference would, in all likelihood, be extended to the adopted child.

On the other hand, if everyone in the family had been collegebound except for Uncle Harry who works in road construction and is considered the family failure, a natural question arises: How would this family feel about a child of below-average intellectual potential or with different occupational preferences than those expected in the family?

Finally, facts about family members' health and causes of death provide an overall family health history and also may say a good deal about the way a family views health, illness, and handicaps. Many of the children awaiting adoption are children with a range of physical and/or mental handicaps. Attaining the health history on the genogram may point to resources the family may have for making a home for a handicapped child.

The demographic data may take the adoption worker a long way toward understanding the family system. However, gathering associations about family members can add to the richness of the portrayal. One can ask, "What word or two, or what picture comes to mind when you think about this person?" These associations tend to tap another level of information about the family as the myths, role assignments, or characterizations of family members come to their minds. It is hard to predict whether the responses to these open-ended questions will be relevant to decision-making around adoption. In a sense, if you don't ask, you'll never know.

The Adoptive Family's Family of Origin

The genogram can be used in the family meetings to explore and share information about all the families of origin that have impact on the nuclear family. Doing the genograms on the adoptive parents' families of origin can serve several functions. First, this process communicates to the adopted child information about the family he or she is joining and enhances the socialization process. The genogram session often stimulates further researches into family history which are carried on outside the family meetings as albums are explored and aged relatives visited. The construction of the genogram objectifies the complex family system and helps orient the child to the family. It becomes a map of who's who and it helps the child identify and connect with the many strangers he or she meets over the first months following the adoption--strangers that are now relatives. This can serve to enhance the child's sense of belonging, not only to the nuclear family, but also to the larger extended family.

Interviewing about the adoptive parents' families of origin may also surface information which may clarify some difficulties or conflicts which are arising in the postadoption adjustment period. This was illustrated in the above case example when we learned about Larry's abusive father and about Janet's lost brother. Sometimes, when such information emerges, it may be a signal for more intensive work with the parents around a particular issue without the children being present. For example, both Larry and Janet needed some extra help in differentiating the current situation from painful events of the past. Larry had completely cut himself off from his father and had no contact with him for ten years. He was encouraged to make contact with his father and was even able, eventually, to talk with him about his childhood and about the abuse. As Larry took charge of his relationship with his father, he became less helpless in dealing with Steve's temper and abusive behavior.

Janet also had some work to do. Her brother's death, so many years before, had in some respects killed her family's emotional system. The loss was never really dealt with and no one ever talked about it. Janet began the belated grieving process with Larry and the worker. She reminisced about her brother, going through every detail of the accident and the funeral, and went to visit the grave, something she had never done. She then involved first her mother and then her father in the grieving process by breaking the family rule and talking about this family tragedy with each of them. She finally organized a visit to the cemetery with her parents. Dealing at long last with this major loss freed her to relate to her new son as himself rather than as a replacement for her brother. An interesting additional change was that her parents, who had been distant and disapproving of the adoption, were now able to move toward Steve and to allow themselves to be his grandparents. This sanction and support from her parents in turn strengthened Janet's sense of entitlement. Although this is highly speculative, it may well have been that, on some deep level, Janet did not feel entitled to have a son, as her parents had lost their only son.[21]

A third outcome of the exploration of the adoptive family's genogram is that the family of origin's attitudes toward the adoption emerge. The strong and enabling support of the extended family is an important part of family building and the genogram can quickly indicate the extent to which the extended family is behind the adoption. Where key extended family members have been disapproving or undermining, the adoptive parents may well feel uneasy and ambivalent about their plans. The opinions of parents and siblings continue to be important in adult life and an atmosphere of disapproval or even lack of understanding can leave the couple feeling isolated and alone in this important venture.

The relationships with the member's family of origin and their attitudes toward the adoption may well be a target for change. Sometimes, the adoptive couple, sensing family disapproval or confusion, withdraws and does not share the experience with the family. This, of course, tends to feed the family's negative feelings and does nothing to bring them closer to an understanding of the couple's wishes and decisions. The adoptive father or mother may be encouraged to reach out to these key family members, to see them alone, and talk with them about what the decision to adopt means. The purpose of such meetings is not to convince the family member of the rectitude of the adoptive couple's decision but to reestablish emotional contact and to make interchange possible. It is important that the adoptive couple take an "I" position with the family of origin, saying, in a sense,

"This is who I am and this is the decision I have made," rather than backing away from the relationship. Whatever the issues around the adoption are between the adoptive couple and their respective families, it is important for the integration of the child into the family that these issues be aired. It may well be that the planning of and the involvement of the family of origin in an adoption ritual, as was discussed in the previous section, may have an important role in surfacing and clarifying the extended family's attitude and in strengthening family cohesiveness.

The Adopted Child's Family of Origin

The whole issue of the adopted child's relationship with his biological family is currently being discussed with considerable heat. The search movement, experiments with open and other forms of adoption, the adoption of older children who know and remember biological family members, as well as a growing conviction about the meaning of our "roots" in all our lives have stimulated a reconsideration of this issue.

The understanding and acceptance of the difference between biological and adoptive parenting enter here, as the major difference is that the child indeed has another family, a biological family, and nothing can alter that fact.

The different ways of structuring adoption and the alternative methods of handling the child's connection with his or her biological family is beyond the scope of this monograph. In the first place, much of this planning and work should be done long before the child goes to the adoptive home. Decisions should be made before the placement concerning how "open" the adoption is to be. Are there salient family figures who have been important to the child? Is it possible to work out ways for the child to remain connected? What safeguards or protections can be set up to make the maintenance of biological family contact workable? All of these questions should be settled before the placement, and the adoptive family, making the commitment to adopt, should be clear about any arrangements or conditions regarding biological family members.

Also, before placement, as complete a genogram as possible should be done for any child coming into care. Many professionals and others interested in identity and continuity have taken the position that every person has both a need and a right to know about their origins. The genogram provides this information to the child and should be available to the child and to the adoptive family. Often the child's genogram provides him or her with positive sources of identification and pride. When adopted people know very little about their family of origin, what they do know is often about dysfunctional aspects of the family, usually related to the family's inability to provide a home or care. However, if more is known, generally an adoptee's family tree is like that of most people, replete with a wide variety of relatives, achieving and nonachieving, sick and well, staid and colorful. Such a breadth of information not only adds to the child's sense of self and his or her potentials in life, it is also helpful in overcoming stereotypes the adoptive family may have developed about the child's biological heritage.

VII. GROUP APPROACHES TO POSTADOPTION SERVICES

Throughout this presentation of methods and techniques for helping families in the first months following adoption, we have set these in the context of service to individual families. This in no way means, however, that such an approach is preferable to working with families, or with adoptive parents, in groups. On the contrary, all of the methods and techniques described can be used very powerfully in a group format.

Commonality is probably the key element in the successful development and use of groups and thus, group services to postadoptive families can be very effective. The common experience of being adoptive parents, the similarity of the issues to be faced, and the problems to be solved develop a powerful cohesiveness in adoptive family groups and promote a strong system of mutual aid. There are many ways of structuring postadoption services. Group services may be primary with individual family meetings on an as-needed basis, or ongoing individual family work may be supplemented by parent-run mutual aid groups of adoptive parents. Other combinations can also be worked out.

Multiple Family Groups

Multiple family groups have been used effectively both in family treatment[22] and in preventive work with nonsymptomatic families[23] This approach to problem-solving can be tailored for postadoption services and can be most helpful.

A multiple family group can be formed of three or four families. These groups should be started around the time of the placement and be a resource for the family from the beginning. The shared experience of adoption forms a strong basis of commonality but the age of the children should be in the same general range. Families of similar structure should also meet together, if possible. For example, single-parent families should probably meet with other single-parent families. Further, the multiple family model is particularly useful for families with children who are adopting. If there are enough families from which to make a selection, some similarity in terms of socioeconomic variables speeds cohesion, although the compelling nature of the shared experience will generally overarch differences.

Meetings should be held on a weekly or bi-weekly schedule at first, but later such meetings may be less frequent. There should be two workers in the group or one worker and a volunteer adoptive parent or pair of adoptive parents who have been through the group experience and have developed the skills through experience and training to help lead the group.

The role of the leaders is not to provide answers, but to facilitate a mutual aid process whereby the families help each other with the issues that emerge. Goals and norms of the group should be clear and should develop out of the process in the early sessions. The leader's role is then to point out to the group when the norms they set are not being followed and when they appear to be straying from their goals.

Goals should relate to the facilitation of the family building process as that is the agency's function and reason for convening the group. How this goal is specified comes out of the group. Norms, as in any group, relate to the usual issues of what can or cannot be discussed, behavior of the children, confidentiality, attendance, roles of members and leaders, etc.

The groups may have structured activities suggested by the worker which enhance the work of the group. For example, all of the tools discussed in this monograph are readily adaptable to group use. Each family can do an Eco-Map and then share these maps with the group. The impact of change on the family can be discussed and group members can help problem-solve around strengthening the family's relationship with its ecological environment. Each family can contribute out of their own experience and can empathize with the stress that is a part of transition and change.

Each family, one at a time, can also sculpt itself and share that experience with the group. Common as well as idiosyncratic experiences will emerge in the sculpting process and are made available for discussion. Genograms can also be presented if the family of origin issues appear to be salient.

One of the major values of multiple family group meetings is that each member of the family has his or her opposite members in the same roles in the other families. It is thus possible to break the group up into different subgroups to talk about different issues. Such subgroups can be fathers, mothers, children already in the family, and adopted children. These subgroups can share problems and perceptions peculiar to their role in the family with an even more heightened sense of alliance. The outcomes of the subgroups meetings can then be brought back into the group. When a volunteer adoptive couple shares the leadership role with the worker, the husband can meet with the fathers while the wife meets with the mothers.

Groups, particularly when there is an important shared status or problem, are tremendously powerful as instruments of support and of change as the effects seem almost to be multiplied by the number of people who are reflecting, working, sharing, supporting, and at times confronting.

Informational or Educational Groups

Throughout this monograph, emphasis on "parent education" and "parent effectiveness training" has been an obvious omission. This is particularly glaring because agencies have often assumed that this is a major postadoption role. This author's conviction is that the use of a strongly educational or parent training role with adoptive parents can have many problematic consequences. First, the agency assuming the role of expert or teacher tends to maintain the stance that the child still "belongs" to the agency and basically still has control over the child. Although before finalization this is technically true, it is essential not to undermine the parents' growing sense of "ownership" and entitlement. Further, the assumption that the parent does not have the knowledge and skills of parenting further detracts from entitlement. Entitlement, in part, comes through a sense of competence and mastery.

Frequently, however, concrete help and information are needed, particularly in the case of special needs adoption because, by definition, some of these children may have needs that are different and require special handling.

The delivery of this kind of help and information through the use of parent groups may diminish the role of agency as authority. In such groups, the agency acts primarily as facilitator, encouraging the development of problem-solving processes, the giving of help, and the sharing of information with the group. Within a strongly cohesive group of peers, the worker can contribute ideas and information to this process without accentuating the authority or control of the agency or undermining the parents' sense of autonomy and competence.

A Mutual Aid Network

Another group approach to the delivery of postadoption service may be through the development of mutual aid networks. Mutual aid networks may develop spontaneously when agencies use group methods in decision making, preparation for placement, and postadoption services. Friendships between adoptive couples may well develop with social, child care, advice, and other kinds of help being spontaneously exchanged. This kind of networking can be facilitated by the agency through the use of a core of experienced adoptive families as volunteers to help families through the postadoption period. This can be a particularly useful model of helping in the adoption of children with special needs, particularly when a family which has coped successfully with a child can offer counsel and support to a family just starting out with a child with somewhat similar needs. This kind of relationship can develop very naturally when fairly early in the process, before a child is placed, the potential adoptive family visits with the experienced family to get a real sense of what it might be like to make a home for a child with special needs.[24]

Mutual aid networks can also be encouraged through agency sponsorship of an ongoing adoptive parents' organization which can develop educational, social and service programs in line with the parents' interests. Such organizations are not only a vehicle for the delivery of postadoption services, but can also be supportive to the agency program in preparation for placement and in the recruitment of families for special children.

VIII. POSTADOPTION SERVICES THROUGHOUT THE LIFE CYCLE

A basic premise of this monograph is that family building through adoption is different than through biological parenting. A further premise is that the more able all of the parties in the adoption are to understand and accept that difference, the greater the likelihood is that the adoption will be successful.[25]

Obviously, the difference between adoption and biological family building is that the adopted child has another family, a biological family, and no matter how early the adoption or how total the cut-off from that family, an important part of an adoptee's identity is deeply rooted in that biological system. If that family is a shadowy unknown, the adoptee's sense of self can similarly be, at least in part, vague and uncertain.[26]

Further, in the adoption of older children, the child has had a life before coming to the adoptive home and has important memories and connections. A total cutting off from this earlier life and an attempt to erase the memories and deny the existence of these early years leaves the child with a major rupture in his or her sense of self and continuity.

The major developmental task for the adoptive family is to integrate the adopted child into the family without repudiating the child's past or denying the existence and importance of the child's biological roots.

The major developmental task of the adoptee is to create a firm and clear sense of self through the integration of the heritage, biological, social and psychological, from two separate families. The task of the agency in long-term postadoption services is to help adoptive family and adoptees with these tasks. Although a range of variety of services may be offered, they center on these two tasks and an agency, in developing its ongoing program, can chart its course with these goals in mind.

In approaching the whole field of long-term postadoption services, however, we move into an area lacking both knowledge and experience. The denial of difference between adoptive and biological parenting in the past has meant that agencies did not believe that adoptive families and adoptees would need special help and thus planned long-term services are new and still relatively rare.[27] As agencies begin to offer long-term services and share their experiences with others, the knowledge and skill required for the provision of such services will develop and be disseminated.

The following tentative suggestions for long-term services grew out of a review of the literature and the author's own experience in working with adoptees and their families, as well as considerable interchange with the adoptee search movement. They are also based on the premises stated above concerning integration and identity formation. They must, however, be considered tentative as we learn more about adoption as a life-long status.

Telling and Sharing Information

One of the special tasks faced by the adoptive parents for which life has given them little preparation is that of telling their child about the adoption and sharing information about the child's biological kin. After all, unless the parents were themselves adopted, this is not a role they saw modeled by their parents. Telling and sharing is a process that goes on throughout the child's growing-up years as different kinds of information are appropriate at different stages in the child's development. Too often the adoptive parent dutifully informs the child of the adoption as the agency has said they should and then feels the task is completed.

In order to share and to tell appropriately, the adoptive family needs two things from the agency: information about the child's biological family and help with the process at key developmental points.

We have discussed the kinds of information that should be available, such as a Life Book for an older child and a full genogram for any child coming into care.

Help with process can be built into long-term service through the offering of discussion groups on "telling and sharing" and on dealing with other adoption issues with adoptive parents at particular times. For example, groups for parents of four- to six-year-olds, for parents of ten- to twelve-year-olds, for parents of teenagers, and for parents of young adults who may be thinking about searching for their biological kin would be useful. If the agency has a strong postadoption service program and maintains contact with adoptive families, offering such services is a natural next step and one which would be welcomed by parents struggling with these issues.

Again, the group approach is particularly useful, as parents who are facing similar situations can share anxieties, concerns, ideas, failures, and successes. Occasionally, a family may have a special concern and they do not feel comfortable about bringing it up in the group and the staff should make time available to meet with parents.

A major purpose of these discussion groups is to facilitate sharing and mutual aid among the parents that every member may be more able to handle issues around adoption with comfort and certainty. Key practical questions are around what to tell, and how and when to tell.

Further, the attitudes held by the adoptive parents about the child's birth family are communicated to the child even if the parents try to hide critical or negative attitudes. These negative feelings become internalized by the child and can have a major impact on his or her self-concept. Because of the importance of these attitudes, a second purpose of the discussion groups may also be to help the parents discuss their feelings about "that other family," their fears and the threat to entitlement that the existence of the biological kin can imply. The sharing of these fears and uncertainties can be supportive and sustaining. A further help in attitude change can be found in the use of audio-visual materials which may enhance empathy toward and understanding of the biological family.[28]

Ongoing Services for Adoptees

One of the important advantages of the ongoing supportive network described in the previous section is that such a network provides opportunities for adopted children to know other children who are adopted. This sharply diminishes a sense of being "the only one who is different." One adoptee told me that in her mid-twenties, when she went to her first adoptee meeting, she could not wait to meet other adoptees, feeling that in a sense they were her brothers and sisters.

For teenagers, when peers are so important and when peer helping is particularly congruent to the life stage, discussion groups for teenage adoptees can be particularly useful. Whether a teenager can allow him- or herself to be involved in such a group will depend largely on the adoptee's and the family's willingness to accept the adoptee status as different. Unfortunately, it may be just those who need the help most who will not be able to reach out for it.

Learning from Adoptees and Adoptive Families

Several kinds of groups of adoptees and parents have been suggested but many adoption agency workers might ask the questions "What would I do with such a group?" "I don't know the answers to the questions they will ask!"

We do not have the answers to these questions because we have not followed enough adoptive families through time to amass a body of good data about what works and what helps. We must learn through doing, we must learn through listening to adoptive families and their children, through listening to adult adoptees, and thus enhance our understanding of these complex human relationships.

The Maintenance of Connectedness

Adoption is changing and, increasingly, the possibility of various forms of open adoption are being considered. Particularly in the case of older children where biological family members or foster parents may have played a key role in the life of a child, it is important to attempt to develop a way to maintain these important connections. Every situation is so different and the strengths and potential dangers so varied that an individual plan describing the form and future of the adoption should be developed in each situation. All the impinging factors must be assessed and weighed and sometimes it will be necessary to take risks to help a child maintain contact with important figures in his or her former life. In weighing the decisions, however, it must be remembered that a complete cut-off also has its risks.

Connections may be maintained through letters, through telephone calls or through visits, and may be frequent or rare, depending on the situation. In making individual plans, it is useful to consider the following guideline: attempt to develop the kind of plan which will help a child maintain a genuine connection without jeopardizing the happiness or security of the adoptive home.

The agency and the ongoing adoption service worker play a crucial role in facilitating the child's remaining connection with the biological family and also in helping the adoptive parents deal with the child's connection with kin. The agency can help in identifying important figures, in facilitating ongoing contact, but also in the setting of limits, the strengthening of boundaries, and in the support of the adoptive family, should they be threatened or overwhelmed. The adoptive family should be free to call on the agency throughout the child's growing up as changing conditions may make alterations in the child's relationship with the biological family necessary. The agency should be responsive to such approaches and be ready to explore options with the adoptive family, the child, or the biological family member. At times, the worker may act as mediator and the successful utilization of that role can lessen the stress experienced by the child if there is tension between the adoptive family and a biological relative of the child.

Long-Term Adoption Services and the Search

At this time, when law and policy regarding adoptees' rights to information concerning the identity of their biological parents is in the process of change, it is hard to define agency roles and functions in relationship to the teenager or adult who is wanting to find the biological family. In fact, the roles and responsibilities of the agency in regard to birth parents, adoptive parents, and adoptees may well be prescribed as a matter of public policy or law. Further, it is impossible to consider a national model for response in this area as laws and procedures differ from state to state. To further complicate this already complex issue, the search movement and the question of open adoption records is highly emotionally charged and adoptees, birth parents, adoptive parents, and professionals have been involved in a very contentious struggle over the entire matter.

Within the context of this confusing transitional period, what can agencies do to help the different members of the adoption triangle? First, workers should be sensitive and available to adult adoptees as they approach agencies requesting information about their origins. Such a request should not be considered a symptom of an emotional problem on the part of the adoptee or the sign of an unsuccessful adoption. In fact, instead of attempting to find hidden meanings in the request, it is important to simply understand and accept the request as a healthy wish on the part of the adoptees to learn more about themselves, to consolidate their identity, and to come to terms with their origins.

Secondly, it is important to attend to and focus upon the needs of the adoptee in discussing the issue. One adoptee, in reporting her experience in approaching the agency through which she was adopted, said that the first response from the worker who saw her was the question, delivered in an anxious and concerned tone, "Do your adoptive parents know you are doing this?" The worker's response to the young woman's wish to search for her birth mother was, "Surely her wounds are healed by now. You wouldn't want to reopen them, would you?" The primary messages communicated by the worker were of protective concern for the adoptive parents and the birth parents. This is not an atypical story.

No matter what the requirements of law and public policy, at least the agency can communicate interest in and acceptance of the adoptee's wish and need to search, even if no concrete help can be offered. One thing an agency can do is to refer the adoptee to the local adoptees' organization. These self-help groups exist all over the country and are now united in a national organization. An adoptee need not be committed to the search in order to join, but can find within the group opportunities to meet and share with others who are dealing with similar issues.

In the discussions of how the law should be changed and how the rights of all should be protected, many professionals have taken the position that social workers and the social agency should remain in a central position between the members of the adoption triangle. In this position, the agency could evaluate the appropriateness of the request, find and contact the birth parent, and if the parent is willing, negotiate a meeting.

Although this may be a useful service to offer those who wish to make use of it, adult adoptees tend to object, very understandably, to once again finding the control of their lives in the hands of social workers and social agencies. Many want to keep control of the search process, to do it autonomously for themselves, and resent the implication that they cannot handle contact with the birth parent without professional help. They object to the passive role taken by the adoptee while the agency arranges everything in almost a repeat of the original adoption. They feel that it is important, if adoptees wish, for them to be able to take the active role and do this themselves.

Agencies may also better serve birth parents and adoptive parents in this uncertain period. With birth parents, the agency may ascertain the birth parents' wishes about future contact with the child and may record this. They may facilitate the birth parents' staying in contact with the agency, maintaining a current address and information about major life changes.

As we have emphasized throughout this monograph, the agency can better serve adoptees and their families by obtaining and making available detailed information about the child's background, and, in the case of an older adoptee, information about the preadoption years.

The whole area of long-term postadoption services has yet to be explored as we venture into this relatively uncharted area. It provides an opportunity for the development of creative practice approaches and new solutions to old and often ignored problems. As the fact that adoption is different is accepted, ways of making it work, ways of understanding and even of capitalizing on that difference, will emerge that can only benefit the many thousands of people who occupy a role in the adoption triangle.

NOTES

1. Helfer and Kempe, 1974; Elmer, 1960; Kempe et al., 1962.

2. Jenkins and Sauber, 1966; Fanshel, 1976; Fanshel and Shinn, 1978; Jenkins, 1972.

3. Hartman, 1979b.

4. Kirk, 1964 and Feigleman and Silverman, 1979.

5. Katz, 1980.

6. Fahlberg, 1980.

7. Ward, 1979.

8. Katz, 1979.

9. Hartman, 1978.

10. Feigleman and Silverman, 1979.

11. Bowen, 1978.

12. Palazzoli et al., 1980.

13. Kagen, 1980.

14. Minuchin and Fishman, 1981.

15. Palazzoli, 1977.

16. Kagen, 1980.

17. Watzlawick et al., 1974.

18. Kagen, 1980.

19. Bowen, 1978.

20. Hartman, 1979a.

21. This model of intervention through helping people actively engage and work through issues with important family members was developed by Murray Bowen. Additional information on this model may be found in Carter and Orfanidis, 1976; Hartman, 1979a; and Colon, 1973.

22. Laquer, 1976.

23. Papp et al., 1973.

24. Tremitiere, 1979.

25. Kirk, 1964.

26. Colon, 1978.

27. Katz, 1980.

28. DiGiulio, 1979.

BIBLIOGRAPHY

Andrews, Robert. "Adoption: Legal Resolution or Legal Fraud," Family Process, 17(3) (September 1978).

Bowen, Murray. Family Therapy in Clinical Practice. New York: Aronson, 1978.

Carter, Elizabeth and Orfandis, Monica. "Family Therapy With One Person and the Family Therapist's Own Family," in Family Therapy: Theory and Practice, edited by Philip Gurrin. New York: Gardner, 1976.

Child Welfare League of America. Standards for Adoption Service, revised edition. New York: Child Welfare League of America, 1978.

Colon, Fernando. "In Search of One's Past: An Identity Trip." Family Process, 12(4) (December 1973).

_____. "Family Ties and Child Placement." Family Process, 17(3) (September 1978).

DiGiulio, Joan Ferry. "The Search: Providing Continued Service for Adoptive Parents." Child Welfare, LVIII(7) (July/August 1979).

Dukette, Rita. "Perspectives for Agency Response to the Adoption-Record Controversy." Child Welfare, LIV(8) (September/October 1975).

Elmer, Elizabeth. "Abused Young Children Seen in Hospital." Social Work, 5 (1960): 98-102.

Fahlberg, Vera. "Attachment and Separation." Project Craft. Ann Arbor, MI: School of Social Work, University of Michigan, 1980.

Fanshel, David. "Status Changes of Children in Foster Care: Final Results of the Columbia University Longitudinal Study." Child Welfare, LV (March 1976): 143-171.

Fanshel, David and Shinn, Eugene. Children in Foster Care: A Longitudinal Investigation. New York: Columbia University Press, 1978.

Feigleman, William and Silverman, Arnold. "Preferential Adoption: A New Mode of Family Formation." Social Casework, 60(5) (May 1979).

Hartman, Ann. "Diagrammatic Assessment of Family Relationships." Social Casework, 59(8) (October 1978).

_____. "The Extended Family as a Resource for Change," in Social Work Practice: People and Environment, edited by Carel B. Germain. New York: Columbia, 1979a.

_____. Finding Families: An Ecological Approach to Family Assessment in Adoption. Beverly Hills: Sage, 1979b.

Helfer, Ray E. and Kempe, C. Henry, editors. The Battered Child. Chicago: University of Chicago Press, 1974.

Jenkins, Shirley and Norman, Elaine. Filial Deprivation in Foster Care. New York: Columbia University Press, 1972.

Jenkins, Shirley and Sauber, Mignon. Paths to Child Placement. New York: Community Council of Greater New York, 1966.

Kagan, Richard M. "Using Redefinition and Paradox With Children in Placement Who Provoke Rejection." Child Welfare, LIX(9) (November 1980).

Katz, Linda. "Older Child Adoptive Placement: A Time of Family Crisis." Child Welfare, 56(3) (March 1977).

_____. "Adoption Counseling as a Preventive Mental Health Specialty." Child Welfare, 59(3) (March 1980).

Kempe, C. Henry et al. "The Battered Child Syndrome." Journal of the American Medical Association, 181 (1962): 4-11.

Kirk, H. David. Shared Fate. New York: The Free Press, 1964.

Laquer, H. P. "Multiple Family Therapy," in Family Therapy: Theory and Practice, edited by P. J. Gurrin. New York: Gardner Press, 1976.

Minuchin, Salvador and Fishman, H. Charles. Family Therapy Techniques, Cambridge, MA: Harvard, 1981.

Palazzoli, Mara et al. "Hypothesizing - Circularity - Neutrality: Three Guidelines for the Conductor of the Session," Family Process, 19 (March 1980): 3-12.

_____. "Family Rituals: A Powerful Tool in Family Therapy," Family Process, 16 (December 1977): 445-453.

Papp, Peggy; Silverbein, Olga; and Carter, Betty. "Family Sculpting in Preventive Work with 'Well Families'." Family Process, 12(12) (June 1973).

Smith, Rebecca. "The Sealed Adoption Record Controversy and Social Agency Response." Social Welfare, LV(2) (February 1976).

Tremitiere, Barbara. "Adoption of Children With Special Needs: The Client-Centered Approach." Child Welfare, 58(10) (December 1979).

Ward, Margaret. "The Relationship Between Parents and Caseworker in Adoption." Social Casework, 60(2) (February 1979).

Watzlawick, Paul; Weakland, John; and Fisch, Richard. CHANGE: Principles of Problem Formation and Problem Resolution. New York: Norton, 1974.

ABOUT THE AUTHOR

Ann Hartman received a master's degree from the Smith College School for Social Work and a D.S.W. degree from the Columbia University School of Social Work. Her career has included practice in public child welfare and family agencies; for eight years she was the executive director of a community mental health clinic. She is currently on the staff of The Ann Arbor Center for The Family.

Dr. Hartman's academic career has spanned five years at Fordham University and ten years at the University of Michigan School of Social Work, where she is Professor of Social Work and faculty director of the National Child Welfare Training Center. She is the author of over 30 articles, monographs, and books, the most recent being Family Centered Social Work Practice, co-authored with Joan Laird, published in 1983 by The Free Press.